The Natural Paint Book

Lynn Edwards and Julia Lawless

The Natural Paint Book

Lynn Edwards and Julia Lawless

RODALE

Rodale Organic Living Books
Executive Editor: Margot Schupf
Art Director: Patricia Field
Copy Manager: Nancy N. Bailey
Copy Editor: Sarah S. Dunn
Editorial Assistant: Sara Sellar

We're always happy to hear from you. For questions or comments concerning the editorial content of this book, please write to:
Rodale Book Readers' Service
33 East Minor Street
Emmaus, PA 18098
Look for other Rodale books wherever books are sold. Or call us at (800) 848-4735.
For more information about Rodale Organic Living magazines and books, visit us at www.rodale.com

First American edition distributed in the book trade by St. Martin's Press

2 4 6 8 10 9 7 5 3 1 paperback

First published in Great Britain 2002 by Kyle Cathie Limited

Library of Congress Cataloging-in-Publication Data
Edwards, Lynn.
The natural paint book : a complete guide to natural paints, recipes, and finishes / Lynn Edwards & Julia Lawless.
    p. cm.
Includes bibliographical references and index.
ISBN 0–87596–914–3 (pbk. : alk. paper)
    1. Painting—Technique. 2. Natural products. 3. Paint mixing. I. Lawless, Julia. II. Title.
    TT385 .E325 2002
    698'.1'0283—dc21
                    2002014803

Text © Lynn Edwards and Julia Lawless
Design and layout © Kyle Cathie Limited
Special photography © Heather Brown, except images listed on page 192

Color separations by Colourscan
Printed and bound in Singapore by Star Standard

Contents

INTRODUCTION

Natural living is the key to the future. Not only do more of us want to minimize the damage caused to the environment by the production and use of the products in our homes, we also want to protect our own health and well-being. We want to feel connected to what has gone before while also looking forward to a sustainable future. In order to accomplish this, we need an alternative to our increasingly highly processed, prepackaged lives, which have distanced us from the natural world.

Top: Natural finishes combine well with natural materials, such as this rough wooden table and pieces of driftwood.
Opposite: Natural paints suit any style interior, from ethnic to country cottage.

This book deals exclusively with natural paints and finishes. There are many books about paints and decorative techniques on the market, but the vast majority refer to paints and finishes that are products of the petrochemical industry, bringing with them associated hazards to health and our environment. We can spend up to 80 percent of our lives inside buildings, yet few people realize that our indoor environment can

be up to ten times more polluted than outdoors. Unknowingly, we may spend the majority of our time surrounded by a complex mixture of toxic emissions from all types of chemical products that we use in our homes and workplaces, including synthetic paints.

The production of synthetic paints also has an enormous environmental impact. Oil—the basis of the petrochemical industry—is a diminishing and nonrenewable resource, and the energy-intensive production of 1 ton of paint from this resource can sometimes produce 10 to 30 tons of toxic waste. Natural paints, on the other hand, are made largely from renewable raw materials such as plant oils, or from materials that are more readily available and in plentiful supply, such as natural earths, clays, and chalk. The ingredients are processed much less, using "soft technology,"

resulting in less waste, energy use, and pollution. The final waste products tend to be biodegradable.

More and more people are realizing that we must take responsibility for our actions and for the choices we make, and are also becoming aware of the very real power we have as consumers. If we keep asking questions about the products we buy and use, we can have an effect on what is offered to us. In relation to paints and finishes, how do we decide which products to use? How do we learn which questions need asking? This book will enable you to make more informed, ethical choices. It explains what paint is and how it is made, both traditionally and synthetically. As a complete guide to home decorating, it also details the full range of natural paints and finishes available, giving recipes and techniques as well as inspirational examples of painted rooms.

Deciding to opt for natural paints and finishes does not restrict the choice that is available for decorating our homes; in fact, it opens up an exciting world of subtle colors, tones, and textures. We can now choose from a range of top-quality commercial products, or opt to make our own paint by following traditional recipes. At one time, all paint was made from natural ingredients, and the expertise in using these products has been built up over centuries. Most traditional paints are easy to make, employ few ingredients, and can be applied using a range of simple techniques. These paints allow for the expression of individuality, create a totally different environment from "conventional" paints, and have pleasant smells instead of noxious ones. Along

with practical instructions on how to prepare and mix traditional finishes such as egg tempera and lime wash, this book suggests ways of using modern eco-friendly latex and casein paints to best effect. It also describes some ways of applying homemade products in creative and decorative ways.

Using such natural products embraces the heritage of painting and acknowledges and appreciates our past. Today, we have the ideal opportunity to combine this traditional expertise with the best of modern production techniques. The ready availability of the raw materials and the knowledge of how to prepare

and use these materials, coupled with our desire to live in safe, beautiful environments, means that we can enjoy creating individual and exciting interiors.

The final chapters suggest ways in which we can turn our homes into a personal sanctuary, a place where we can escape from the stresses of the modern world and feel nourished by our surroundings. Extending the principles of natural organic living throughout the house, a range of design ideas and advice helps provide inspiration for every room. By simply using color, light, texture, and space to their best effect, we can transform our interiors into healthy and uplifting places in which to live.

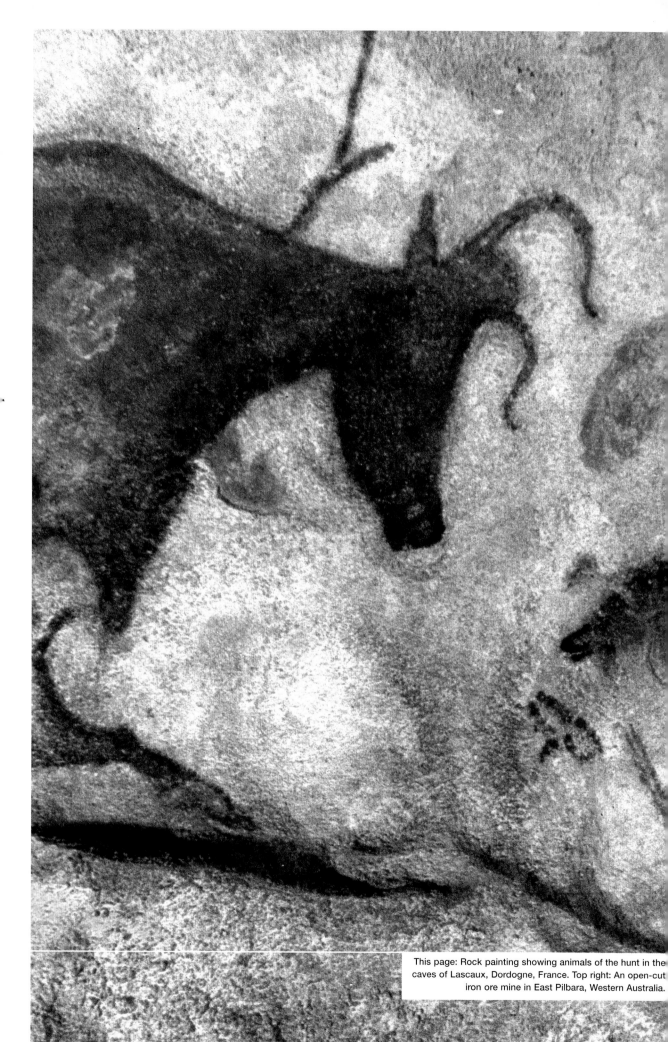

This page: Rock painting showing animals of the hunt in the caves of Lascaux, Dordogne, France. Top right: An open-cut iron ore mine in East Pilbara, Western Australia.

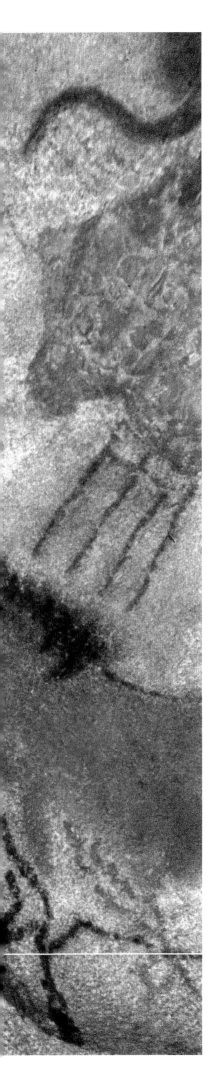

THE STORY OF PAINT
REDISCOVERING OUR HERITAGE

Palaeolithic Cave Paintings

"We have invented nothing...none of us can paint like this!" These were the words of Picasso on viewing the Palaeolithic paintings at Lascaux and Altamira. This was how a twentieth-century genius paid homage to the heritage that had lain undiscovered for millennia. Here were techniques such as perspective, toning, and shading, which we had thought were relatively modern inventions, used by ancient man with great expertise, despite having a relatively limited paint palette.

To look at the history of paints and finishes is to view human accomplishment in a microcosm. Characteristically, we have brought to the development and use of decorative materials the same attributes that we bring to everything: inquisitiveness, innovation, endeavor, and inspiration. Yet, as we shall see, the results of these enduring human tendencies are not always positive.

The earliest known surviving workings with paint are possibly the petroglyphs of dots at Jinmium in Australia, which are perhaps as much as 50,000 years old. The recent discoveries at Grotte Chauvet near the Ardèche gorge in France are thought to be more than 30,000 years old, while those at Bhimabetaka in India may be more than 25,000 years old. The best known, but later, cave paintings of Altamira in northern Spain and Lascaux in southern France were created some time between 15,000 and 20,000 years ago. Wherever they are found, Paleolithic cave paintings display similar characteristics, both in terms of the materials used and the execution of the paintings and drawings themselves.

Excavations at Lascaux have found that earth pigments were ground in hollows in the floor using heavy animal bones and stones. Analysis has shown that the pigment-rich clays were combined with water, animal fat, blood, and albumen to make very sophisticated paints. The paint palette consisted of white (chalk and lime), black (soot and charcoal), and the reds, browns, and yellows of natural earths. Sticks of charcoal and "crayons" of pigment-rich clay were used to outline paintings (just like Rembrandt). The paints were applied with combinations of brushing, using the chewed ends of twigs, feathers, and animal hair; smearing and dabbing, using the hand and pads of mosses and lichen; and spraying through hollow bones and reeds—primitive air brushes. The painters then proceeded to paint pictures of stunning power and beauty that are as remarkable today as they must have been when first executed.

If animal fats and water were the first paint mediums, then tree saps were the next. From a North African conifer, *Tetraclinis articulata*, a sap was extracted and boiled to make an alcohol-based paint—sandarac. It was so widely used during the ensuing millennia that sandarac became the generic name for paint. Boiling the sap of pine trees produced turpentine, and from the pine nuts came an oil. Together with wax extracted from bees' nests and shellac (the secretions of the Indian lac insect, *Laccifer lacca*), there now existed the raw materials for an exponential diversification of paint manufacture and the creation of varnishes and oil finishes.

Recent discoveries have shown that the people who made some of the Lascaux cave paintings would travel up to 25 miles (40 kilometers) to obtain their materials. Bearing in mind the hazardous conditions under which early humans lived and their relatively short life span, painting must have been extremely important to them. It was not only

the walls and ceilings of the caves that were painted but tools, clothing, and bodies as well. Three theories have been developed, by extrapolating from primitive tribes that still exist today, as to why so much precious time and energy was expended in this way:
– *For pleasure or recreation, or to tell a story*
– *Sympathetic hunting magic, based on the belief that to paint a picture of the hunting and killing of a beast helps to achieve it in actuality*
– *Artistic symbolism, the representation of the unknown, the natural and supernatural forces, vital and ever-present in our existence*

These early existing works display all the basic elements that we shall find in the succeeding story of decorative finishes—ingenuity and effort in the development of basic materials, techniques, and tools, together with imagination and a desire to express oneself.

EARLY CIVILIZATIONS

Around 10,000 to 12,000 years ago, the population of the Earth had increased sufficiently for communities to begin developing into what we would recognize as civilizations. Humans had changed

from hunter-gatherers who lived in caves to farmers who constructed dwellings of mud, wood, and stone. With a more settled lifestyle, time not spent on providing food and shelter could be expended in other ways. This diversification of activity brought the discovery of new materials, and experimentation with these brought new uses. Any surplus goods produced could be exchanged with other people, and so the art of trading developed.

The "cradle of civilization" became the Mediterranean area from the "Pillars of Hercules" (the Straits of Gibraltar) extending over the coasts of the Mediterranean, to the Tigris and Euphrates valleys in present-day Iran, Iraq, and Arabia. All around this region, developing civilizations were trading surplus goods, skills, and people. They also came into conflict, and those with more resources, better access to materials, and a greater native genius grew faster and established empires. Ultimately, these empires were replaced by newer, more active and vibrant civilizations. The most developed of these created the greatest range of, and uses for, paints and finishes.

Opposite page: Cave painting of horses in the caves of Lascaux, Dordogne, France.

Far left: A Venda chief's hut showing traditional decorations in Zimbabwe.

Left: *Echinops ritro* is one of many plants used in the manufacture of paint.

THE EGYPTIAN EMPIRE

Around 5,000 years ago, the people of Egypt were the first to create a truly great civilization. At its apex, the Egyptian Empire was 20 percent larger than China and, over a period of 3,000 years, the ancient Egyptians discovered and developed most of the arts and sciences we recognize today. As remarkable innovators, they examined all their natural materials for all possible uses. A material such as a gum or an essential oil could be used to make incense, perfume, paint, or a protective covering for furniture. Myrrh gum, for example, was used in a range of perfumes, medicines, and cosmetics and was also used as an incense ingredient. Oil from the famous cedar of Lebanon was used not only in the preparation of incense but also as an insecticide, and for the preservation of furniture, buildings, coffins, and human bodies (the oil was injected into corpses as part of the mummification process). The Egyptians were also great miners, and they uncovered an ever-increasing range of raw materials. The city of Ammonium was founded on the sites of huge deposits of ammonium sulfate, a material that enabled waxes and gums to be made soluble in water.

The enormous number of buildings that the Egyptians erected provided huge opportunities for decoration. The city of Thebes would have been the largest building site in the world at that time, and we are fortunate that the Egyptians have left us precise records of their daily life in their paintings, papyri, and hieroglyphs. Surviving inscriptions and wall paintings also depict the roles of their gods and rulers, for the Egyptians had a highly developed and sophisticated spiritual life, and their connection with divinity was ever-present. Apart from using their knowledge of raw materials, paints, and artistry purely for aesthetic reasons, the Egyptians frequently honored their gods and goddesses with beautifully executed murals and decorative finishes. At Karnak (in Thebes), for example, the Hypostyle Hall of the temple dedicated to the god Amun was built with more than 100 huge pillars carved to look like papyrus ascending from a primeval swamp to the vault of the sky, where the ceiling was painted brilliant blue with golden stars. It is estimated that there were 80,000 workers in hundreds of workshops, working with materials from all over the known world brought down the Nile to Karnak by barge.

For the houses of the wealthy and for places of worship, lapis lazuli and azurite were ground to make blues, while heated galena (lead ore) produced a range of colors from white through red. Greens were made from crushed malachite and chrysoprase. A further range of blue and green tones was also made from the acidic corrosion of copper—the verdigris would be produced by suspending copper plates over ammonia, vinegar, or urine, or by covering them in grape skins. Oils, waxes, resins, mastics (the finest from the island of Chios), eggs, milk, lime, turpentine, and alcohol were all used to make a wide variety of paints and finishes, each with different properties and potential applications.

It is also estimated that around Karnak there were hundreds of farms with grazing for over 1 million cattle. It is not surprising, then, that milk paint, along with paints based on milk, lime, and natural earths (materials readily available and inexpensive), became a predominant medium in decorating the more humble Egyptian adobe homes.

Opposite: The coffin of Pasenhor (1070-661 B.C.).
Below: Tomb painting of Sennedjem and his wife, who are shown worshipping the gods of the underworld.

This page: Natural paints give an individual feel to an otherwise plain interior. Pages 16 to 17: Fresco at the Villa of Mysteries, Pompey

CLASSICAL GREECE

The Minoan civilization on ancient Crete borrowed and developed skills from the Egyptians. During the second millennium B.C., they were building and painting beautiful buildings. Their culture was largely destroyed around 450 B.C. by the natural disasters that followed the volcanic eruption on Santorini, and by subsequent invasions by the Mycenaeans from modern-day southern Greece. Little was known about the glory of Minoan culture until the discovery by Sir Arthur Evans, in the early 1900s, of the palace at Knossos 3,500 years after it had been built. What was revealed astonished the world at the time—the striking brilliance and modernity of some of the earliest fresco painting ever discovered.

By the first millennium B.C., Egyptian culture was declining, but Egyptian workers and knowledge had passed to the rising culture of Greece. Like the Egyptians, the Greeks colored all their monuments. The great bare columns of marble on the Acropolis in Athens were, in fact, originally painted. Only small remains of this sort of painting can be detected anywhere in the ancient world, as they have been eroded by the ravages of time.

THE PHOENICIANS

The Phoenicians were the world's great travelers at this time. They sailed from the Mediterranean to India, Africa, Arabia, the Far East, and as far north as the British Isles. Their boats were protected with a paint of sandarac, castor oil, and red lead—the first seaworthy paint. They carried materials, skills, and knowledge between cultures.

THE MEDES

In southwest Asia, the Medes, an ancient race succeeded by the Persians, painted the seven concentric walls of the city of Agbatana in ancient Persia, from outer to inner, painting the first five white, black, scarlet, blue, and orange, and plating the last two silver and gold. These seven colors represented the seven great heavenly bodies. This must have been an absolutely immense undertaking. The great temple of Nebuchadnezzar at Borsippa was colored in the same way, indicating the significance of the attachment of color to the supernatural.

THE ROMAN EMPIRE

The destruction of early civilizations in the Mediterranean basin, either by natural disasters, as at Knossos, or by periodic invasion, has in most places left us with only fragments on which to base our knowledge of the materials and techniques used. However, the Vesuvian eruption during the first century B.C. has left intact a superb memorial to the skills that had been developed by the Roman Empire. At Pompeii we can glimpse the full glory of their artistry. There we find evidence that the range of colors had grown, as had faux techniques like trompe l'oeil, marbling, and graining. Pliny, writing later, would bemoan the profusion of new colors that the expansion of the Roman Empire had brought into use: purple made from the murex shellfish, cinnabar (vermilion) from mercury-rich ore, the plant colorant indigo imported from India, and other blues made from pulverized enamels.

The decline and fall of the Roman Empire in the West during the fourth and fifth centuries A.D. led to the centuries-long hiatus in the further development of paint finishes. The center of knowledge in the Mediterranean area moved to Byzantium, renamed Constantinople after Constantine the Great, and ultimately to become modern Istanbul. Unfortunately, Constantine, on his conversion to Christianity, ordered the closure or destruction of all signs of worship of the pagan gods, thereby losing for posterity much that we could have studied. Constantinople later became the center of Islamic culture, which would spread its own particular artistic and scientific genius throughout the Mediterranean world. However, the Muslims too had no time for relics, monuments, or images to a Christian god, and they would destroy yet more potential sources of information.

India and China, meanwhile, were continuing to use water-based paints and varnishes made from shellac and from the lacquer tree (*Rhus verniciflua*), and were largely unaffected by the great changes that Europe was undergoing.

THE RENAISSANCE

The Renaissance in Europe and the admiration of all things Greek and Roman brought with them the rediscovery of the paints and techniques of the ancient world, as well as the development of new ones such as painting with oils. It also brought with it the separation of art from craft. Until the Renaissance, the same words were used for "decorator" (i.e., house and wall painter) as for "artist." It is only relatively recently that we have talked of some decoration as art and promoted it

to an exalted position. In English, of course, we use the term "painter" to refer to someone who executes both house and wall painting and artistic work, and in Italian the word "artigiano" once meant "craftsperson" as well as "artist."

During the Renaissance, the production of decorative masterpieces and an ever-increasing passion for ostentation flourished. Ordinary people, meanwhile, continued painting their homes in the simple but effective paints of lime or milk, as they had done for centuries. In addition to mineral and earth pigments, dye pigments were made from plant and animal colorings. For example, a blue foam known as "Fleurée de Pastel" was extracted by leaving a dye bath of the herb woad to evaporate; the dry residue was mixed with lime wash for use on walls and ceilings, or with chalk for use on canvas. The French word for woad—"pastel"—became the name we now use for drawing chalks.

A RETURN TO SIMPLICITY

By the seventeenth century, with the rejection of the teachings of the Catholic Church came an outright objection to opulent decoration and adornment. In Europe, simpler and more functional finishes came back into vogue. Many families also left the "Old World" at this time and set sail for America, taking their skills and beliefs with them. After the English Civil War in the 1640s and the subsequent restoration of the monarchy, many Quakers, a puritan sect, left Europe and founded Pennsylvania in 1682, taking with them their belief in craftsmanship and simplicity. A Quaker sect known as Shakers, led by Ann Lee, joined the earlier colonists in 1774, and they took with them their ideas of maximum utility, simplicity, and minimal decoration. They decorated houses and furniture using simple milk paints, natural oils, and waxes. These finishes have an austere beauty, still much admired today.

THE IMPACT OF OIL

The eighteenth and nineteenth centuries also brought with them advances in science and technology, and these were subsequently applied to paint production. Travel and increasing affluence brought new influences and a flowering of styles, which could be enjoyed by the rich. The movement from the land to the ever-burgeoning cities during the Industrial Revolution increased a separation between the simple local decoration of the countryside and the ornateness now becoming apparent in cities such as London and Paris, where new products and materials were greeted with enthusiasm. During the second half of the nineteenth century, this lust for novelty received the greatest impetus it had ever had with the drilling for oil.

Crude oil, or petroleum, had been known and used for centuries. It was found in small pools, streams, and shales, where it had naturally seeped up through layers of rock. Native Americans had used it for making paint and also for magic and medicine. In 1859, Edwin Drake drilled the first oil-producing well in Titusville, Pennsylvania, and the world began to change. At first, the main impact was on the whale oil industry, as kerosene replaced its use in lamps, but 37 years later, in 1896, the automobile was invented. The demand for oil began to increase, and many more countries started to look for their own sources. Inevitably, humans brought to this material those same tendencies of innovation, inquisitiveness, endeavor, and inspiration that were earlier applied to painting and artistry. Scientists investigated the properties of this new material, just as raw materials had been analyzed and utilized by preceding generations. In addition to being used as a fuel, oil was scientifically studied, and gradually the numerous chemicals composing petroleum were isolated. In the scientists' search for uses, new substances that did not previously exist in nature were made. These new materials, such as plastics and paints, were seen as positive innovations, and there followed an increasing dependence on oil products.

When the "modern" paint manufacturing industry began during the latter half of the nineteenth century, producers convinced people to change from traditional paints by promoting the idea that their new products were more durable. This was despite the fact that some ancient paints have lasted for thousands of years. Although these new paints were initially much more expensive, people were persuaded to buy them, and painters changed their practices accordingly. By the twentieth century, the massive petrochemical industry had not only changed our lives but also come to dominate them. It created great wealth for some, became a factor in energy crises and war, and, perhaps most seriously, impacted on our environment.

Coupled with this growth of wealth and industry, the twentieth century also saw great changes in the way in which we relate to the natural world, in terms of both its resources and our spiritual connection with it. Our innate desire, even if unconscious, to acknowledge essential forces has been replaced by the "religion" of consumerism, with its insatiable and unsustainable consumption of our planet's raw materials. A consumer culture, by its very nature, can generate only discontent and a restless search for that certain something we can never quite attain. It is not surprising, then, that for many of us, life at the beginning of the twenty-first century does not feel as good as it could.

CHOICES FOR THE FUTURE

Living in the modern Western world, we are rarely aware of the source or properties of the products we use. This is quite different from the way our ancestors related to the world around them and, consequently, they experienced connections that we have largely forgotten. In rediscovering natural paints and finishes, we begin to revive these

Opposite: A New England shaker interior. Above: An artist shown mixing color in a medieval manuscript.

lost associations and thus perceive our connection to nature and our environment in a new light.

To everything there is a reaction, and cultures do change. In the 1960s and 1970s, the seeds of change were planted by writers like Rachel Carson (*Silent Spring*), James Lovelock (*GAIA: A New Look at Life on Earth*) and E. F. Schumacher (*Small Is Beautiful*). They and others voiced growing concerns that our actions would have detrimental consequences, both immediate and in the longer term. One choice is to review where we stand at the beginning of the twenty-first century, to take responsibility, and to act accordingly. Sometimes the damage that humans have inflicted on the planet can seem overwhelming, and the constant buzz of the marketplace, where new and shiny things dazzle us, can be hard to resist. Lao Tzu, in the *Tao-te Ching*, famously said that "A tower of nine storeys begins with a heap of earth. The journey of a thousand li starts from where one stands." Whether we have built our own ecofriendly tower and now want to decorate it, or whether this is just the first step on our own personal journey of discovery, we

Above: A temple to modern consumerism—the Trafford Centre, Greater Manchester, England.

are all part of a movement of people who are awakening to our power as consumers. Moreover, the process of making choices, where the real costs and the real value of things are understood, is a process by which we can rediscover and experience a greater integrity and more nourishing relationship with the Earth.

This page: Malachite provides a paint pigment.
Top right: Cedar of Lebanon is a source of oil

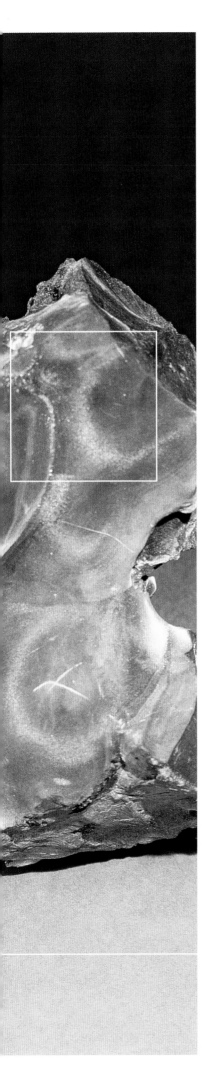

A MATTER OF CHOICE

One way for us to create a spiritually nourishing and physically sustainable future out of our present-day culture of consumerism is to be aware that each of us can make a huge difference just by making conscious choices about how and where we spend our money. This chapter is designed to provide information about the environmental and health consequences of the type of paint we choose to decorate with.

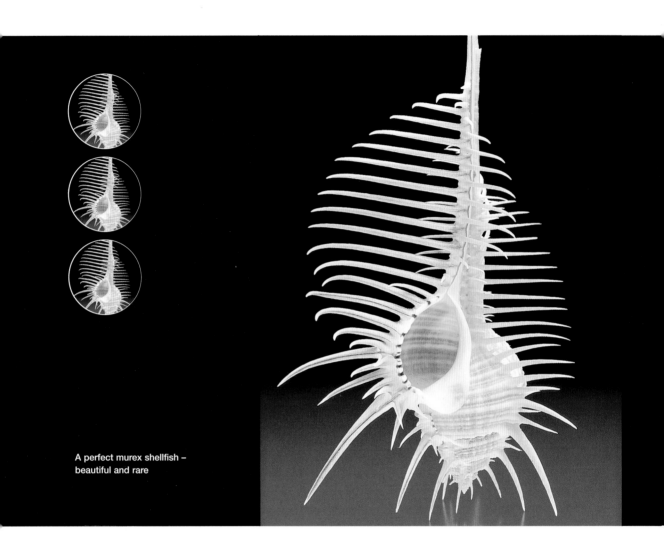

A perfect murex shellfish –
beautiful and rare

The impact of this one single area of choice is significant—in the United States alone, over 1.2 billion gallons (4.5 billion liters) of paint are used each year. The following list provides some guidelines for choosing sustainable decorating materials. Wherever possible:
– *Choose raw materials that originate from renewable resources.*
– *Choose materials that are abundantly available, preferably locally.*
– *Minimize the amount of energy used to extract, process, and transport the products.*
– *Keep production simple and low-tech.*

– *Avoid substances that are toxic to the user or the environment.*
– *Produce only those waste products that will biodegrade easily.*

WHAT IS PAINT?

Paint is a way of applying and holding a film of color to the surface of a material or object, sometimes for purely decorative reasons. Additionally, it might also be used to protect and preserve the material to which it is applied. A small amount of paint can protect a manufactured building material and extend its useful life, and therefore any paint that performs well in this respect can be seen to be of

benefit to the environment.

In its basic form, all paint consists of a coloring pigment and a binder; to these, solvents and additives are mixed in.

PIGMENTS

Color is provided by pigments, which normally come in the form of a powder. These can be:
– *Organic: a substance containing carbon. Carbon compounds form the basis of all living organisms and their remains, including petroleum and other fossil fuels.*
– *Inorganic: a substance based on other elements, usually mineral, including metals and silicates.*

– Natural: a substance produced as a result of the planet's natural processes.
– Synthetic: a substance produced by human invention, usually as a result of human ingenuity in combining individual compounds in order to imitate particularly desirable qualities of natural materials.

Examples of natural organic colored pigments are plant and insect colors such as reds from madder or cochineal, generally extracted through a dye-making process. Alizarin, the predominant red pigment in madder root, was first synthesized in 1868. The color obtained from madder root itself is made up not only of alizarin but also of many other pigments, including blue or sometimes yellow tones, demonstrating that, in nature, there are no solid blocks of color but rather subtle combinations and transitions, which are usually naturally harmonious. Although beautifully pure and translucent, these natural pigments tend not to be light-fast, and will fade or alter with time.

Examples of natural inorganic colored pigments are natural earth pigments (generally oxides of iron suspended in clay) and mineral pigments (colored rocks and crystals), mined from the earth and then heated and roasted to produce a variety of colors. It is difficult to achieve a flat expanse of a pure color by using natural earth and mineral pigments, since the shades of these can vary a great deal depending on their source. In addition, their crystalline structure means that when they lie on the surface of paint, light is reflected from them in many directions, giving vibrancy and depth to the finish.

Some pigments used in synthetic paints are derived from natural heavy metals such as chromates, and in the past natural pigments like arsenic and lead were used to color paint. These are illustrations of how "natural" does not always equate with "nontoxic;" in fact, some of the strongest poisons we know of are natural substances.

Examples of synthetic organic colored pigments are products of the petrochemical industry. Synthetic dyes, first created in 1771, are much brighter, more light-fast, cheaper to produce, and more predictably uniform in color than naturally occurring materials.

Our choice of colors now is likely to be made purely on the basis of what suits the room and its furnishings. In earlier times, however, it was commonly understood that different colors carried specific messages and had symbolic meanings. Graves have been unearthed where bodies have been painted in a ritualistic manner or lumps of pigment have been interred with the deceased. To the ancient Egyptians, yellow symbolized power. Later, used in a halo around depictions of Christian saints, golden yellow denoted sanctified glory. In the West, white is the color of innocence, yet in China it signifies death. Red is associated with blood, the life force, and with vital, active, assertive energy. The word "hematite" (the source of many red iron oxide pigments) derives from the Greek word "haima," meaning "blood."

In addition to providing color, pigments can also give the paint opacity, or covering power. The most widely used "hiding" pigment is titanium dioxide, an expensive but extremely opaque—and therefore highly valued—white pigment. Titanium dioxide is a natural mineral, which, in its raw state, is given a buff color by its iron content. Purification of titanium dioxide is energy-intensive and accounts for the majority of the energy consumed in producing paint. Titanium dioxide also has the reputation of being a cause of pollution due to

A piece of lead ore from Dumfriesshire, Scotland.

Above: Wax extracted from bees' nests has been used for thousands of years to create beautiful finishes.

Below: Lapis lazuli can be ground to produce a blue pigment.

the sometimes poor waste-disposal management of the hydrochloric acid that is used during the purification process and of the extracted iron oxide. Legislation and research have led to production methods that may now be less harmful to the environment. There are also health concerns about the inhalation of titanium dioxide in its dry powder form. It is vital to wear a face mask when sanding down old paintwork; in fact, the inhalation of any type of dust always should be avoided, if possible.

Less expensive, "non-hiding" pigments or fillers are used to fill out the gaps between the more precious colored pigments. Fillers include chalk, talc, and clay.

Different pigments also have additional effects on properties of a paint, such as flow and film formation. The type and the amount of pigment in a paint determines whether the finish will be matte, glossy, or somewhere in between. Proportions are also dependent on the strength of the binder (the fluid in which the pigment is suspended), but matte paint usually contains around 70 percent pigment to 30 percent binder. Once the paint is dry, a good quantity of pigment remains exposed on the surface, giving it a matte quality. In some

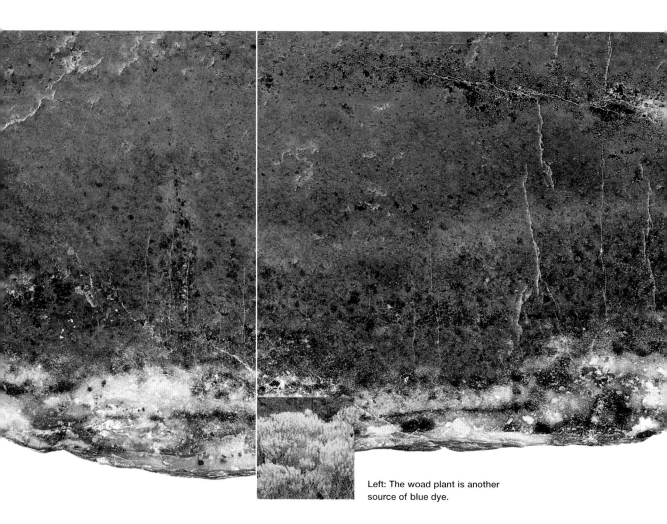

Left: The woad plant is another source of blue dye.

Left: Lead ore from Dumfriesshire, Scotland. Above: Pollution caused by modern paint manufacture is a cause of concern.

circumstances, weak binders are valued because they allow the qualities of a natural pigment to dominate the finish.

By contrast, glossy paint has around 20 percent pigment to 80 percent binder, which means that, upon drying, the most predominant ingredient would be the binder, giving both a glossy and a more durable surface to the finish.

BINDERS

A binder is the fluid in which the pigment is suspended. When liquid, it acts as a carrier for the color during application; when dry, it also acts as a glue to hold the color in place. There are several types of binder, both synthetic and natural, and each will result in different properties of the paint film. Each type of binder can be used alone or in combination.

SYNTHETIC BINDERS

One type of paint binder, used for almost a century, is a group of alkyd resins based on synthetically modified vegetable oils. Other synthetic binders, such as polyvinyl acetate and acrylic, have arisen as by-products of the oil-refining process and, like synthetic pigments, are another relatively recent development.

Petroleum, or crude oil, is a naturally occurring material. It is the product of decaying animal and plant remains that have become buried under thick layers of rock during the past 600 million years. Because it took so long to form, petroleum is considered to be a precious and nonrenewable resource. As discussed on page 18, this fossil fuel has been essential for the technical and industrial development of our societies. At present rates of consumption, however, some

estimates expect this resource to run out in about 50 years.

Crude oil consists principally of a mixture of hydrocarbons (molecules of carbon and hydrogen linked together in various shapes). Various processes in the oil refinery separate the components of this mixture from each other. The first of these processes is called fractional distillation, whereby crude oil is heated and sent into a tower. The vapors of the different components condense on collectors at different heights in the tower, thus being "fractionated." The lighter fractions, including gasoline, are in greatest demand, and so the heavy hydrocarbons are subjected to further processing, involving heat, pressure, and certain catalysts, in order to break them down into smaller molecules. This secondary process is known as "cracking." These processes require the input of vast amounts of energy and complicated technology to achieve their end products. They also inevitably result in the production of undesirable waste materials. The production of each can of paint can leave behind 10 to 30 cans of waste.

There are many examples of how petroleum has polluted the environment, not only around the refineries but also during extraction and transportation. Many of the chemicals made from crude oil have since been proved to be toxic pollutants in themselves, and the end products of this industry are also polluting, since plastics and artificial resins do not decompose but persist in our environment long after they have lost their usefulness.

NATURAL BINDERS

Natural binders have been in use for thousands of years. Examples of natural binders are plant oils and resins, natural latex, casein, milk, eggs, cellulose, and animal glues.

To take plant-based binders as an example, one can see that the raw material is still growing. Not only is this resource renewable, it is also absolutely vast. Approximately 187 billion tons of plant biomass is produced each year. The energy source for this production is sunlight, which is used by plants through photosynthesis, and the raw materials for this plant chemistry are water and carbon dioxide.

It is possible to decide to manage the production of these raw materials in an ethical and sustainable fashion. Some natural paint producers use raw materials that have been grown organically, i.e., without the use of artificial fertilizers and pesticides, and relying instead on maintaining fertile soils

and healthy growing conditions.

Some raw materials, such as tree resins, can be harvested by sustainable methods and support indigenous people at the same time. The production of dammar resin, a binder used in some natural paints, has already ensured the protection of part of a rain forest in Sumatra, along with the income and way of life of the people who live there. Dammar is a renewable resource because trees do not have to be cut down in order to harvest it, and it has become an economically viable alternative to the destruction of forests containing tropical hardwoods in order to make plywood.

In Vietnam, tapping pine trees for their resin is often women's work. It not only provides them with an income but is also an incentive for the community not to over-exploit the wood in pine plantations for fuel, which is already a scarce commodity there. Developing countries could be supported by a growth in demand for renewable natural raw materials, and any dangers of exploitation could be avoided by applying the principles of fair trade.

Some natural paint companies are researching the large-scale production of plant material, breathing new life into our own agricultural industry, and finding sustainable alternatives to our current reliance on a resource that will soon be exhausted. One such company is funding research that will enable farmers not only to grow traditional dye plants but also to process the raw materials on site, thus cutting down on transportation costs.

Some natural binders can be extracted in a more or less pure state and require little refining, and therefore the production processes have low energy consumption. For

example, linseed oil is simply pressed from the seeds of the flax plant. If desired, it can then be further processed in a relatively simple way by heating it to produce linseed stand oil. Cellulose, the most abundant organic compound on Earth, requires more energy to extract and refine; some natural binders go through even more complex production procedures, like making an alkyd resin from soybean oil, which involves breaking the raw material down into smaller molecules.

Inevitably, there are waste materials from natural paint production, but these differ from the chemical waste products of synthetic paint in that they will biodegrade. Over the course of millions of years, nature has learned to reintegrate natural waste products into closed ecological cycles. Each of the millions of compounds produced in nature is balanced by an associated natural enzyme that can break it down, enabling it to decompose and be recycled through the planet's natural systems. As long as we do not interfere too much in natural processes by altering materials beyond the point whereby they can be recognized by nature (using genetic modification, for instance), we can work within our closed ecological system.

Below: Resin tapping.

	Synthetic	Natural
Production	This is unsustainable because the raw material is running out and is nonrenewable.	This is sustainable because the raw materials are either in plentiful supply or regrowing.
Energy	It takes a large amount of energy to extract and refine the raw material.	It does not take a lot of energy to extract the raw materials, and they are refined in simple processes.
Waste products	These and the end products are chemically synthetic. They are not recognized by nature and therefore cannot be reabsorbed.	These and the end products are biodegradable, and the carbon dioxide and water they produce are reabsorbed into living plants and trees.

SOLVENTS

Solvents, or thinners, are combined with the pigment and binder mix to make it into a usable consistency. Examples of synthetic solvents are denatured alcohol, isoaliphatic hydrocarbons (fossil fuel-derived solvents that have been purified to eliminate their more noxious properties), and turpentine substitute. Examples of natural solvents are turpentine, plant alcohol, and citrus thinners.

All of the above solvents are volatile (i.e., they will evaporate easily at normal room temperatures), and they all contain carbon in their makeup. They are therefore classed as Volatile Organic Compounds. VOCs are a source of concern because they can be harmful both to human health and to the wider environment, although, in general, natural VOCs are less harmful than synthetic ones.

THE DANGERS OF SYNTHETIC VOCS

Most of us are familiar with the smell of fresh paint and have noticed that glossy paints can be particularly potent. This is because they tend to contain the highest proportions of solvent—sometimes up to two-thirds of a can of glossy paint or varnish is designed to evaporate into the atmosphere. Many of us have experienced the symptoms of short-term exposure to VOCs when painting our homes. These can include headaches, nausea, dizziness, fatigue, and blurred vision. The consequences for those who work as painters and decorators and who therefore have long-term exposure, are, however, more serious.

In Australia, the Occupational Health Officer of the Operative Painters and Decorators Union, Noni Holmes, coined the term "painters' syndrome" to describe the effects that solvents used in synthetic paints can have on those exposed to them in the medium and longer term. Solvents are absorbed through both the lungs and the skin, and the results can include asthma, emphysema, dermatitis, and effects on the central nervous system such as memory loss. In Denmark, "painters' dementia" is a recognized industrial disease.

In the United States, two environmental health consultants, Dr. Otto Wong and Robert Morgan, reported to the U.S. National Paint and Coatings Association that painters experience significant increases in both lung and bladder cancer.

These findings were echoed by the World Health Organization's International Agency for Research on Cancer (IARC), which is considered to be the preeminent authority on the carcinogenic potential of chemicals. In 1989, the IARC classified painting as a high-risk occupation.

Home painters and decorators do not experience such high exposure to solvents, and our bodies can usually do a good job of dealing with low levels of toxins, but increasing numbers of people are suffering from illnesses such as asthma and multiple chemical sensitivity, the symptoms of which can be brought on or worsened by exposure to paint fumes. It is not just the initial exposure to fresh paint that is of concern. Most of us spend most of our time indoors, both at home and at work, and most of the internal surface areas of buildings are painted. Low levels of VOCs can continue to be emitted from paint for up to 5 years after application, and studies have shown that the indoor environment is now up to 10 times more polluted than the external environment. Paint is not the only culprit, however: Modern building materials and furnishings can also emit toxic VOCs, including formaldehyde (which is not a solvent). The U.S. Environmental Protection Agency estimates that indoor pollution from VOCs is responsible for more than 11,000 deaths a year in the United States from cancers, kidney failure, and respiratory problems.

Several countries have now begun to legislate on the permitted limits of the VOC content of paints. In reaction to this, and recognizing that the market is changing, some of the large manufacturers of synthetic paints have started to change their formulations and to label their products "Low VOC" or "Zero VOC." These are positive moves, but the negative aspect is that the consumer might equate "Zero VOC" with "safe," when, in fact, there are other additives and the whole concern of surrounding ourselves with synthetic substances to consider.

VOCs also have an impact on our external environment. Once released into the atmosphere, they react with other pollutants. One of the known results of this interaction, especially on warm, sunny days, is the production of low-level ozone, or smog. Government legislation on VOCs, however welcome, is concerned only with reducing the quantities of these photochemically reactive compounds in the atmosphere. Other VOCs are not limited under these laws, even though some, such as formaldehyde, are known carcinogens.

Finally, we have to consider the wider effects of releasing synthetic VOCs into the atmosphere. Synthetic solvents are mostly derived from fossil fuels, and the plants from which these fuels were originally made died millions of

years ago. This means that releasing carbon compounds from synthetic solvents is a one-way process, just the giving off, because the original plants are not there to reabsorb it. Such a process goes against the laws of nature and contrasts starkly with the closed ecological system of natural solvents (see below).

THE DANGERS OF NATURAL VOCS

VOC legislation has also affected the manufacture of natural paints, since natural solvents are also volatile and some of them are classed as toxic. Turpentine, for example, which is distilled from an oleoresin from the pine tree, is a skin, eye, mucous membrane, and upper respiratory tract irritant. It may also cause skin sensitization, central nervous system damage, gastrointestinal problems, and urinary tract infections. Again, the home painter and decorator is unlikely to experience chronic exposure to turpentine, but the importance of adequate ventilation should be emphasized when working with any kind of solvent. Some users are adversely affected by high concentrations of citrus thinners, and some natural paint companies have compromised on this point by using synthetic solvents such as isoaliphates, currently produced from petroleum. So, not all the ingredients in natural paint are necessarily nontoxic or 100 percent environmentally friendly.

THE BENEFITS OF NATURAL VOCS

Pine and citrus trees continuously release volatile organic carbons into the atmosphere, which creates the scent of a pine forest or orange

grove. Using turpentine or citrus thinners as solvents is simply a more concentrated form of this natural process. Natural solvents release compounds from plants that are still cultivated and therefore absorb equivalent amounts of compounds from the atmosphere. Unlike the use of petrochemicals, this balanced and closed ecological cycle of giving off and reabsorbing means that nature's natural processes are not affected.

CHOOSING A VOC-FREE ALTERNATIVE

As a result of the concern over the harmful effects of solvents, there has been a growth in the market for water-based paints. This has had a positive effect on the release of solvents into the atmosphere at the point of application. Research and development in the paint industry as a whole has now made it possible to manufacture water-based paints that contain no solvent whatsoever. This has, however, sometimes resulted in more complex paint formulations, involving a greater number of additives such as detergents, anti-foaming agents, and emulsifiers, albeit in minute quantities, so the paints may still be harmful.

An advantage of water-based paints is that the paint can simply be washed out of the brush under a faucet instead of needing a solvent to remove it. This activity should not be encouraged, however, as it only increases the burden on our water treatment systems. Even natural paint companies recommend using old newspaper to remove as much paint as possible, then washing only the last remains from the brush. They also suggest leaving any unwanted paint to dry before disposing of it properly.

Top to bottom:
Sunflowers, flax, and
poppies are renewable
sources of oil.
Although natural, lead
is a toxic ingredient of
some paints.
Reseda produces a
yellow dye still used
today.

ADDITIVES

If synthetic paint manufacturers listed the additives contained in a can of their paint on its label, as most natural paint manufacturers do, it would probably appear something like the lists of seemingly indecipherable ingredients on the labels of processed foods. When these lists first appeared, we were interested—and alarmed—to see the extent of additives that the manufacturers were including in most of our foods. We became more knowledgeable about what these numbers meant, and put pressure on the manufacturers to produce an increased range of processed foods with fewer additives in them.

In the same way, we have a right to know what is in the paint we use in our houses so that we can make an informed choice between natural and synthetic products. Most natural paint manufacturers openly declare the ingredients in their products on their labels and in their accompanying literature. Synthetic paint manufacturers will provide lists of ingredients only if requested, but they do not put them on their cans. Public pressure on this issue might force synthetic manufacturers to declare their ingredients and even to produce safer paints.

Paint additives include:

– Thickeners.
– Surfactants: These reduce the surface tension of a liquid, allowing it to foam or penetrate solids.
– Antifoaming agents.
– Driers: these help some paint formulations to dry by acting as catalysts to natural processes such as oxidation and polymerization. There are health concerns even over the siccatives used in some natural paints, however, because of the problems of their inhalation as dust when paint is being sanded down.
– Biocides: These toxic additives contain both preservatives, to keep bacteria from growing in the paint can, and fungicides, to discourage mold growth after application. Some natural paints have a shorter shelf life because they use safer alternatives, such as essential oils or food-grade preservatives.
– Plasticizers: These prevent dried paints from becoming too brittle and may be added to latex paint; examples include phthalic acids, or phthalates, which are suspected hormone disrupters.
– Coalescing co-solvents: These may be added to synthetic latex paints to aid film formation qualities; they are particularly unpleasant and noxious.

PERFORMANCE

NATURAL PAINTS FOR WOOD AND METAL

These tend to take longer to dry than their synthetic counterparts, relying more on natural processes such as the evaporation of water, oxidation, and polymerization, so more time and care may be needed for successful results. Paints that contain linseed oil, especially when used on wood, dry so slowly that they are able to penetrate deeply into the wood's pores. In this way, the paint forms a proper bond with the material underneath, rather than lying as a separate coating on the surface. Plant-based products also tend not to dry really hard but to remain flexible, sometimes for years, moving with the natural expansion and contraction of the wood. If applied correctly, therefore, the plant-based paints should not lift or peel.

SYNTHETIC PAINTS FOR WOOD AND METAL

These generally contain additives that help to make the product quick and easy to use. The paint flows on easily and dries rapidly to form a hard, smooth film, but it is more liable to crack with time, especially when applied to wood.

NATURAL WALL PAINTS

Size-based and casein-based paints have given natural wall paints the reputation of not being as washable as their synthetic counterparts. Modern ecopaints, however, have come a long way since their beginnings in the 1970s. The application of research and technology means that washable, even scrubbable, wall paints based on natural ingredients are now available. It is worth remembering, however, that not all areas in every home need to be washable.

SYNTHETIC WALL PAINTS

These use paint binders made from petrochemicals, which have the qualities of synthetic fibers and plastics. This makes them hard-wearing and long-lasting, but it also means that they are statically charged and so actually attract dust to their surface.

NATURAL FINISHES

The long-term economies of using natural products are especially apparent when applied to the treatment of wooden floors or

exterior woodwork. When it is time to apply a new surface coat, there is no need to strip off all the old paint. Cleaning and a light sanding are all that are required before a new topcoat is painted on. Natural finishes are microporous, allowing the treated material to breathe. This means that any moisture in the substrate will be able to evaporate through the surface coating.

SYNTHETIC FINISHES

These tend to trap moisture underneath the surface. The moisture may eventually bubble up and break through the

paintwork, or it may remain trapped and cause problems such as mold growth and rot. Impervious coatings, no matter how hard wearing they are, are of no use if the structure is rotting away underneath.

THE REAL COST OF PAINT

Natural products have the reputation of being expensive. This is not true of all natural paint products, but one of the reasons why most are more expensive than their synthetic counterparts is that, until now, their production has been on a relatively small

scale. We can, however, expect renewable raw materials to play a much larger role in a widespread range of areas in the immediate future, and this will include the paint industry. An increase in demand for renewable ingredients may initially push prices even higher, but this should settle down once the supply increases to meet the demand. As with the recent massive growth in the organic food market, however, there will be dangers of exploitation and unethical practice to consider.

Synthetic products, including paint, contribute to "sick building syndrome" (a group of symptoms, such as headaches, eye irritation,

The light-reflecting qualities of natural paint
produce a rich, textured quality particularly
suited to large areas of flat color

and lethargy, that may be experienced by workers in air-conditioned offices), and companies occupying afflicted offices have witnessed a higher incidence of staff absence due to sickness. Synthetic paints may seem more economical initially, but we need to take into account the phenomenal cost of researching cures for cancer, asthma, allergies, and other health problems, all known to be related to chemical pollution, as well as the costs of illness. When we consider all these factors, we might see that prevention (choosing natural paints) is cheaper than curing the ill effects of synthetic paints.

For some, choosing to decorate naturally might be a personal contribution toward reducing the impact we have on the planet. For others, such as those who are among the growing number of people who experience extreme chemical sensitivity, it is part of a real need to create a space in which to live and work in safety and good health.

MAKING YOUR CHOICE

The process of choosing paints that are safe for the environment and for the end user from the variety of natural products now available can be simplified by defining your own priorities and being aware of which compromises you are willing to make. Very broadly speaking, one could list types of paint in terms of the hazards they pose (from best to worst option) as:
– Lime wash, size-based paints, and casein
– Water-based plant and mineral paints
– Solvent-based plant and mineral paints

– Water-based synthetic paints
– Solvent-based synthetic paints
Choices can then be made within this scale according to your own circumstances.

Your overriding concern may be to minimize the impact of your decorating materials upon the environment. Some guidelines for choosing sustainable materials appear on page 22 at the beginning of this chapter. You could, in some circumstances, consider choosing not to paint at all but to use plasters colored with natural pigment instead. You could even decide to leave some surfaces undecorated.

The type of room or surface you are intending to paint may determine your choice. The need for durability and low maintenance may exclude the use of the most simple, traditional paints that top the above list (see chapter 6 for details).

Manufacturers of natural paints will be making compromises—or not—on your behalf, and some are more public about their ethics than others, but in all cases it is useful to read the information given to you (either automatically or upon request) by the manufacturer. This might include a list of ingredients contained in the product, which is particularly important if you suffer allergic reactions to certain substances and so want to avoid them, or if you are a vegetarian or vegan to whom some of the ingredients of certain natural paints are unacceptable (see the appendix for full listings of ingredients).

You may have to make compromises of your own, too. If, for example, your priority is to use a certain color that is not achievable by using natural pigments, you might be happy to compromise by using a paint made from renewable raw

materials but tinted with synthetic pigments. Another example concerns acrylic, which, although synthetic, is a very strong binder— you may decide that the use of a small amount of this precious resource to improve the stability of pigment in an otherwise naturally based product is justifiable. Similarly, you may consider the minimal use of isoaliphates as solvents to be acceptable.

Our hope is that the commitment of natural paint companies to developing safe and sustainable alternatives should make the need for these compromises a temporary issue only.

TERMS USED BY MANUFACTURERS TO DESCRIBE THEIR PAINT

LOW OR ZERO VOC
As we have discussed, reducing VOCs is a positive move, but it is not the whole answer.

ORGANIC
Although some natural paint producers use some organically grown ingredients, "organic" can be applied to any substance containing carbon, that is, any living thing, plant or animal, and its remains. This definition includes petrochemicals.

TRADITIONAL, HERITAGE, AND HISTORICAL PAINTS
Strictly speaking, these are size-based paints, linseed oil paint, lime wash, and modern adaptations of these original formulations. You need to look at the ingredients.

TRADITIONAL COLORS
Sometimes these are synthetic reproductions of colors that would originally have been made from natural pigments.

Above: Natural pigments used in paint production. Opposite: Steel wool and sandpaper are necessary tools for some projects.

NATURAL PAINT RECIPES

The following recipes are simple combinations of a few common raw materials, many of which you might find in your kitchen cupboard or refrigerator. Others can be obtained from specialty suppliers.

A basic introduction to some of the materials, along with a few guidelines on preparing and working with them, is followed by a selection of recipes. None of these recipes is set in stone. Variations on them have been developed over the years according to regional traditions and locally available materials. As with cooking, once you have grasped the basics, the recipes simply provide a starting point from where you can proceed according to your personal taste and the materials you have on hand. Make a note of the proportions that you use in each recipe so that you can make up another batch of the paint if it is successful. Above all, have fun experimenting!

THE INGREDIENTS

WHITING

SAFETY: Always wear a mask when handling powders.

Whiting needs some preparation to ensure that the mixing of the dry powder with water is smooth, even, and successful.

Place the whiting in a bowl or bucket and add enough cold water to cover. There is no need to stir. The following day, the whiting will have "fattened" (swollen up with the absorbed water) and there will be a layer of clear water on the surface. This should be poured or skimmed off.

NATURAL PIGMENTS

SAFETY: Always wear a mask when handling powders.

Natural pigments need some preparation to ensure that the mixing of dry powders with water is smooth, even, and successful. If the pigment seems a little coarse, it can be ground to a finer powder in a mortar and pestle that has been set aside for this purpose. This, plus overnight slaking, will help you to avoid bursts and streaks of dry pigment in the paint finish.

If they are to be used in a water-based recipe, then pigments need to be slaked overnight. To do this, put some pigment in a bowl and mix in enough cold water to make a smooth runny paste, then let the mixture stand. Some pigments do not mix easily with water; these may be slaked in a little alcohol, such as vodka, to make a smooth, runny paste. There is no point in slaking "glimmer" pigments.

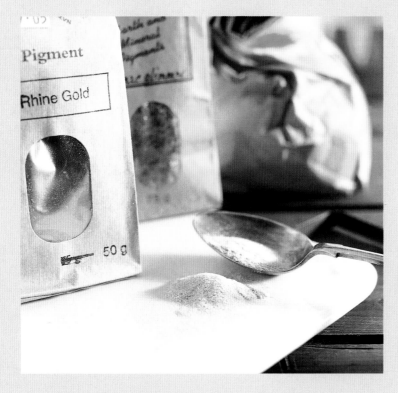

Opposite: French chalk.
Left and above:
Glimmer pigments

Pigments are often used in very small amounts that are very hard to weigh on kitchen scales. For quantities below 1 ounce (25g), the amounts are therefore given in teaspoons or tablespoons for ease of measuring.

EARTH AND MINERAL PIGMENTS

The properties of natural earth pigments can vary, depending on the composition of the particular piece of earth from which they were mined. Earth pigments are composed of clay containing different forms of iron oxide, plus other minerals such as manganese. It is the various combinations of these ingredients that determine the natural color of the pigment. Some pigments are roasted after extraction in order to produce further colors.

As a guideline, green earth pigment has a weak tinting strength because it is composed mainly of clay, but most of the other natural earth pigments, such as ochers, siennas, and umbers, are medium-strength colorants. Umbers and ochers tend to be quite opaque, and their high clay content can tend to thicken the paint. Siennas, by contrast, are more transparent. Red iron oxide, as its name suggests, has a high iron oxide content and is a powerful tinting pigment.

White pigments are obtained from titanium dioxide and zinc oxide. Both ultramarine blue (a powerful colorant) and ultramarine red (less powerful) are made from sodium aluminum silicate (clays), burned at high temperatures with sulfur. A green pigment is obtained from chromium oxide. Manganese violet is a powerful colorant, while ultramarine violet is less powerful.

Spinels are hard crystalline minerals or precious stones that have been ground into a fine colored powder—lapis lazuli, for example. These are, by their nature, rare and expensive, and so consequently some of the blue, green, and violet pigments you buy today are likely to be synthetic versions of these traditional products.

PLANT AND INSECT COLORS

Cochineal, made from the bodies of dried wood lice found on a cactus, is used to color some types of red pigment. Delicate, light-sensitive, plant dyes are used by some

Opposite: Oils (clockwise from top, tung oil, poppy seed oil, sunflower oil, and linseed oil). Right: Oils bring out the natural beauty of wood floors.

natural paint manufacturers in some of their products. Examples of these are kesu blossom (orange), krapp root (red), madder (reds and browns), reseda or weld (yellow to olive green), and woad and indigo (blue).

"GLIMMER" PIGMENTS

By-products of the metal industry, these fine granules of gold-, bronze-, and silver-colored material can be used to create fantastic metallic effects.

EXPERIMENTING WITH PIGMENTS

As you experiment with a few recipes, you will discover that different types of pigment have different qualities.
– *Some are much more opaque than others.*
– *Some have very intense coloring, some weaker.*

– *Some have the effect of drying the binder or will absorb more oil than others.*

This variation between pigments is one reason why it is a good idea to paint one or more sample boards before attempting the finished piece. A sample board could be a stiff piece of cardboard, section of plasterboard, or area of wall that can easily be painted over. This practice will give you a feel for how different paints behave as they are being applied. Casein powder and borax paint and lime paints, for example, appear to be transparent when you are painting them on but then dry opaque. Their color also dries several shades lighter than it appears when wet. The same is true of size-based paints.

A sample board will also tell

you whether you have the right proportions of binder to whiting and pigment in your mix. Too much whiting or pigment and the paint will powder off when dry; too much binder and the hard, dry paint will crack and flake off.

OILS AND WAXES

SAFETY: All oils and waxes are flammable products. Keep them away from sources of ignition, along with any rags or paper that have become impregnated with these materials. Do not crumple rags and paper up into balls and throw them in the trash because they can spontaneously combust. Instead, dispose of small amounts of paper by burning them in a fireplace or backyard, if possible, and soak rags in a bucket of water before washing them in detergent and hot water for reuse.

Left: Beeswax. Above: Turpentine and citrus thinners.

LINSEED OIL

Considered to be the most useful oil, this is extracted from crushed flax seeds. It produces an elastic binding agent that is the main base for many natural oils, stains, paints, and varnishes. Boiled linseed oil, or linseed stand oil, has been heat-treated and will dry more quickly than the raw oil. This is the oily ingredient most frequently referred to in the following recipes, but other oils may be substituted. Poppy seed, safflower, sunflower, and tung oils are all used in natural finishes.

BEESWAX

This is a valuable traditional finish for wooden surfaces.

SOLVENTS

SAFETY: Care must be taken when using solvents, even these natural ones. Ensure that there is plenty of ventilation at all times. Remember that, like oils and waxes, solvents are all flammable products. Keep them away from sources of ignition and apply the same safety rules as for oils and waxes.

Citrus thinners and turpentine are plant-based products commonly used as solvents, thinners, and cleaners.

BINDERS

The binders used in these recipes include casein powder (with borax), cellulose glue, rabbit-skin glue, and gum arabic.

LIME MATERIALS

SAFETY: Lime is a highly caustic alkali and must be handled with care. Protect your skin and eyes by wearing gloves and goggles, and wash any accidental splashes immediately. People with very sensitive skin or dermatitis should be especially careful. Seek medical advice in the event of persistent inflammation due to contact with lime. Small splashes in the eye can be washed with copious amounts of water. In addition to this, seek medical help if more than this gets into the eyes.

Do not swallow lime and do not eat, drink, or smoke in the same area as lime. If you get a splash in your mouth, rinse it well with water and drink plenty of water. Seek medical attention if more than a splash is ingested.

Lime putty and hydraulic lime are both sustainable building and decorating materials. In the lime-production cycle, limestone (calcium carbonate) is burned in a kiln, driving off carbon dioxide and water. A hard, white substance known as quicklime (calcium oxide) is left behind. When this is added to water, the reaction, known as "slaking," is so violent that the water starts to boil. Once the reaction is complete, the resulting material is lime putty (calcium hydroxide), which must be stored in an airtight container. Less-pure limestone, contaminated with clay, forms hydraulic lime when burned, and this cannot be slaked to make lime putty because it sets by reaction with water—hence the name "hydraulic."

Once lime putty is exposed to the air—in the form of a lime wash, for example—it reabsorbs carbon dioxide to become calcium carbonate (limestone) again. Hydraulic lime also turns into limestone through the same process and by reacting with the water in the lime paint.

The unecological aspect of large-scale lime production is the high amount of energy needed for the burning stage of the process. Lime putty and hydraulic lime have been in use for thousands of years and, historically, production was originally on a smaller scale according to local need and using locally sourced lumber to fire kilns.

KITCHEN INGREDIENTS

The following kitchen items are all useful for making paints: glycerol, honey, lemon juice, skim milk or quark, tea, vinegar, beer, eggs.

Opposite and below: Many different kitchen tools and ingredients can be used in the production of natural paints and finishes.

EQUIPMENT LIST

Scale
Measuring spoons
Measuring cups
Metal spoons
Buckets
Bowls of various sizes
Whisk attachment for an electric beater
Electric hand-held beater
Colander
Strainer
Cheesecloth
Saucepan
Double boiler
Large (4–5 inch/10–12.5 cm) paintbrush
Medium (2–3 inch/5–7.5 cm) paintbrush
Long-haired masonry brush
Artist's paintbrush
Stiff brush (shoe brush)
Stencil brush
Flat brush
Lint-free rags
Small sponge
Large sponge
Steel wool/fine sandpaper
Pan scourer
Mortar and pestle
Protective gloves and goggles

WALL SURFACES

Walls have different porosity and absorbency, depending on their finish, and the coverage and drying times of the paints and washes given in this book will vary depending on the porosity and absorbency of the surface to which they are applied. Highly porous and absorbent surfaces are unpainted plaster and plasterboard; a less porous and absorbent surface is a wall that has already been painted; and a nonabsorbent wall would be one sealed with a glossy surface like eggshell or acrylic glaze.

Above: A mortar and pestle can be used to grind certain natural pigments.

Opposite: The use of natural paints in the bedroom creates a serene and restful environment.

RECIPES FOR WALL PAINTS AND FINISHES

QUARK

Dried quark, or milk curd, is the basis of casein paint. Quark is actually a very low-fat soft cheese available at specialty gourmet stores, but you can also produce it yourself from two simple ingredients.

INGREDIENTS
Juice of a lemon
1 quart (1 liter) skim milk
This makes 18 ounces (500g) quark

Method
Put the milk into a large bowl and stir in the lemon juice. Leave it overnight in a warm place to curdle. Separate the curds from the whey by pouring the mixture through a cheesecloth placed in a colander. The curds remaining in the colander are known as quark.

Quark is a basic ingredient of several natural
paint recipes and colorwashes.

QUARK COLORWASH

A simple but weak binder, quark can be used to produce thin colorwashes on walls and bare wood. The weak binder allows the qualities and colors of natural pigment to shine through.

INGREDIENTS
9 ounces (250g) quark (about 1 cup)

**2 tablespoons natural pigment
(see pages 36–39)**

The amounts given should cover approximately 43 square feet (4 square meters).

Uses
This colorwash is suitable for absorbent walls. Although it will not rub off, it is not washable.

Method
Slake the pigment (see page 36). Put the quark into a bowl, then stir in the slaked pigment. Add enough to make a usable colorwash. Stir regularly during use, as the pigment will tend to settle out.

Application
Once mixed, this wash needs to be used fairly quickly, or it will go sour and start to smell. Once dry, however, any smell disappears.

Apply the colorwash following the instructions on page 102. The colorwash dries in 1 to 2 hours, although this is very dependent upon atmospheric conditions and the surface to which it is applied.

Wash brushes and tools in warm, soapy water.

Quark colorwash produces a subtle finish that is
equally suited to modern and traditional interiors.

QUARK AND OIL GLAZE

Adding oil to quark makes for more sophisticated glazes because subsequent layers do not dissolve the ones beneath. There is room for a lot of experimentation as you discover the beautiful effects of layering one color over another.

INGREDIENTS
9 ounces (250g) quark (about 1 cup)

¼ cup (50ml) linseed oil

3 tablespoons (20g) natural pigment (see pages 36–39)

The amounts given should cover approximately 43 square feet (4 square meters).

Uses
This glaze is suitable for absorbent walls. It can be wiped clean but is not washable. This glaze is ideal for giving a more durable finish to walls painted with casein powder and borax paint (see page 56), which cannot be wiped clean without this extra coating.

Method
Slake the pigment (see page 36). Put the quark into a bowl, then whisk it with an electric beater while drizzling in the oil very gradually. Next add the slaked pigment. Dilute the mixture with water to a glaze consistency.

Application
Apply a layer of glaze with a large paintbrush and let it dry thoroughly for 2 to 3 hours before applying the next thin veil of color. The oil content of this glaze will take several days to dry thoroughly.

Wash brushes and tools in warm, soapy water.

Layers of quark and oil glaze can be built up to produce an elegant and sophisticated finish.

QUARK AND LIME PAINT

Numerous variations of milk and lime mixes have commonly been used as paint in the United States and Europe. Both ingredients are cheap and plentiful and, when mixed together, make a very effective paint. The casein in the quark reacts with the calcium in the lime to form calcium caseinate, which binds itself both with the pigment in the paint and with the surface that is painted.

SAFETY: Lime is a highly caustic alkali and must be handled with care. See detailed advice on page 41.

INGREDIENTS
9 ounces (250g) quark (about 1 cup)

1 ounce (25g) strained lime putty (about 2 tablespoons)

2 ounces (50g) lime-tolerant natural pigment (about ½ cup; see advice on page 62)

The amounts given should cover approximately 22 square feet (2 square meters).

Uses
This paint is suitable for absorbent walls. It is very durable and can be wiped clean. If thinned further, it can be used as a colorwash. The paint can also be used on bare wood, where two coats will result in an opaque finish that lets the texture of the wood show through.

Method
Slake the pigment (see page 36). Put the quark into a bowl and stir in the lime putty. The consistency will change quite remarkably from something resembling cottage cheese to a usable paint. Add the slaked pigment.

Application
Apply two or three coats to walls with a large paintbrush; the texture of the brush strokes will be evident. Stir regularly during use. The paint is dry to the touch in under an hour and hardens fully overnight. It can then be recoated the next day.

If used on wood, apply two coats with a medium paintbrush, letting the first coat dry thoroughly before recoating. When the topcoat is dry, buff it to a soft sheen with a lint-free cloth.

Wash brushes and tools in warm, soapy water.

Quark and lime paint makes a suitable finish for a set of children's furniture.

QUARK AND BORAX PAINT

Mixing quark, which is acidic, with an alkali like borax turns it into a stronger binder that will hold not only more pigment but also some whiting. The result can be either an opaque wall paint with good covering properties or a thinner colored glaze, depending on the proportions of water, whiting, and pigment that you use.

INGREDIENTS
9 ounces (250g) quark (about 1 cup)
1½ tablespoons (10g) borax
¼ cup (50ml) hot water
½ cup (100g) prepared whiting
    (see page 36)
1 ounce (25g) natural pigment
    (about ¼ cup; see pages 36–39)

The amounts given should cover approximately 22 square feet (2 square meters).

Uses
Walls need to be absorbent. Although it will not rub off, this paint is not washable.

Method
Slake the pigment (see page 36). Put the quark into a bowl. Stir the borax into the hot water in the top part of a double boiler. Dissolve the borax in hot water. Let the borax mixture cool before stirring it into the quark. Combine this binder with the prepared whiting and slaked pigment.

To achieve a glazed effect, thin the paint with more water.

Application
It is a good idea to paint a sample board to check your proportions. Once the paint is dry, rub your finger across the surface. If the paint powders off, you need to add more borax mixture. If it dries to a hard, glassy surface that cracks and flakes off, you need to add more whiting or pigment.

Prime walls with a thinned first coat of paint or just a mixture of binder and water. Let this dry before applying the prepared paint with a large paintbrush.

It may be necessary to adjust the thickness of the paint by adding more water. Paint that is too thick or dries too quickly will tend to powder off.

Wash brushes and tools in warm, soapy water.

Quark and borax paint can be used as an opaque
wall paint or thinned to produce a more
translucent glaze.

CASEIN POWDER AND BORAX PAINT

Casein powder is simply the natural protein component in the milk or quark used in previous recipes, which has been extracted and dried. In this recipe, the acidic casein powder is mixed with alkaline borax, and the result is a really strong and glutinous glue-like binder to hold the pigment and whiting. The paint dries to give a velvety matte surface, which can be rich with vibrant color.

This is a paint that has been used for many centuries – notably by the Shakers, who used casein paint to decorate their furniture and interiors.

INGREDIENTS
**5 ounces (150g) casein powder
(about 1¼ cups)
1 quart (1 liter) cold water
2 ounces (50g) borax (about ½ cup)
1 cup (250ml) hot water
18 ounces (500g) prepared whiting
(about 2¼ cups; see page 36)
5 ounces (150g) natural pigment
(about 1¼ cups; see pages 36–39)**

The amounts given should cover 130 square feet (12 square meters), or much more if used as a thin wash.

Uses
This paint is suitable for indoor use on absorbent surfaces. The finish is not washable but, when dry, is traditionally oiled or waxed so that it can be wiped clean. The quark and oil glaze recipe (page 50) is suitable for this.

Method
Slake the pigment (see page 36). Put the casein powder into a bowl and pour in the cold water. Let it soak overnight.

The next day, stir the borax into the hot water in the top part of a double boiler. Gently heat the mixture, stirring, until the borax has dissolved. Take the pan off the heat and let the borax mixture cool.

Mix the casein into a smooth, lump-free paste using an electric beater. When the casein is smooth, add the borax solution and continue to mix. The result will instantly be a thick, jelly-like glue. Mix in the prepared whiting. Don't worry too much if the paint is very glutinous at this stage. Let it stand for half an hour before stirring it again.

Add the slaked pigment and adjust the thickness of the paint by adding more water. The paint should feel like light cream.

Application
It is a good idea to paint a sample board to check your proportions.

Once the paint is dry, rub your finger across the surface. If the paint powders off, you need to add more casein powder and borax mixture. If it dries to a hard, glassy surface that cracks and flakes off, you need to add more whiting or pigment.

If your walls are very absorbent, thin a little bit of the paint down and use this to prime the wall. Then apply several coats of the paint with a large paintbrush, using large, criss-cross brushstrokes. Stir the mixture regularly during use. Each coat dries in about an hour.

Wash brushes and tools in warm, soapy water.

The velvety finish of casein powder and borax paint makes it suitable for both walls and furniture.

SOFT SIZE-BASE PAINT

Size-base paint has both a history and a reputation. It is basically a reversible finish; in other words it can be washed off. In fact, it has to be washed off before repainting takes place because it is not easy to paint over size-base paint. Historically, this was an advantage when painting moldings on ceilings and cornices because there was never a build-up of successive layers of paint to obscure the delicate details.

These days it may seem like an inconvenience to have to wash off the old paint before applying the new, but it is not actually that arduous a task, particularly if this recipe is used over only small areas. This interior paint finish is very beautiful, soft, and matte, and the natural pigment grains that lie on the brush-textured surface reflect the light to produce variation in color and tone. This finish will also give perfect authenticity to renovated properties.

INGREDIENTS
2¼ cups (500ml) water

2 ounces (50g) rabbit-skin glue granules (about ½ cup)

2¼ pounds (1kg) prepared whiting (see page 36)

2 ounces (50g) natural pigment (about ½ cup; see pages 36–39)

The amounts given should cover about 86 square feet (8 square meters).

Uses
This paint is suitable for use only on absorbent walls. Size-base paints have a delicate existence: Although they should not rub off, they are not washable and will mark easily with grease or water.

Method
Slake the pigment (see page 36). Put the water in the top part of a double boiler, heat until warm, then add the glue granules. When the granules have dissolved, turn off the heat and leave the mixture in the pan overnight. In the morning, the solution will have set, but gentle heating will melt it again. Do not put the pan on high heat because you risk overheating the glue.

Mix the whiting well, ideally with a whisk attachment on an electric beater, while gradually adding the warm glue and the slaked pigment until mixed thoroughly.

Application
It is a good idea to paint a sample board to check your proportions. Once the paint is dry, rub your finger across the surface. If the paint powders off, you need to add more rabbit-skin glue. If it dries to a hard, glassy surface that cracks and flakes off, you need to add more whiting or pigment. This is also a good time to check the color of your paint, since it dries several shades lighter. Adjust the mix if necessary. The paint should be the consistency of a thick latex paint and can be thinned with water.

Prime the wall with a very thin wash of rabbit-skin glue (made from 2 ounces (50g) glue granules

(about ¼ cup) to 4 cups (1 liter) water. Let this dry and then apply the paint, using a large paintbrush. The ridges formed by the brush will remain very prominent in the paint finish, so this might influence the type and direction of brush stroke you decide to use. Try to work quickly, keeping a wet edge. One coat should be sufficient, and it will take about 2 hours to dry.

To remove old distemper, use a large brush to wet the paint with water, then wipe off the paint with a large sponge, rinsing it frequently in clean water.

Wash brushes and tools in warm, soapy water.

Size-base paint dries to a lighter finish, as shown by the sample board above right, which shows wet and dry versions of the same paint.

CELLULOSE GLUE PAINT

Cellulose, a plant-based glue, is available from specialist suppliers, often sold as a natural wallpaper paste. A filler of whiting is added to this binder to make a reversible paint, which can be soaked and washed off. It remains more elastic than rabbit-skin glue, and this means that you can build up two or three thin layers without pulling off the first coat, as would be the case if you tried this technique with soft size-base paint (see page 58).

INGREDIENTS

- **3 tablespoons (20g) cellulose glue powder**
- **4 cups (1 liter) water**
- **7 ounces (200g) prepared whiting (about 1 scant cup; see page 36)**
- **3 tablespoons natural pigment (see pages 36–39)**

The amounts given should cover approximately 86 square feet (8 square meters).

Uses

This paint is suitable for only absorbent walls. It is not washable.

Method

Slake the pigment (see page 36). Make up the glue by sprinkling the powder into the water, letting it stand for 30 minutes, then stirring the mixture well.

Add the cellulose glue to the prepared whiting, along with the slaked pigment, and stir thoroughly. Let the mixture stand for another 30 minutes. The paint should be the consistency of thick sour cream; thin it with water if necessary.

Application

It is a good idea to paint a sample board to check your proportions. Once the paint is dry, rub your finger across the surface. If the paint powders off, you need to add more cellulose glue. If it dries to a hard, glassy surface that cracks and flakes off, you need to add more whiting or pigment.

Prime the wall with a very thin wash of cellulose glue, made from 1½ tablespoons (10g) cellulose glue powder to 4 cups (1 liter) water. Let this dry, then apply two or three coats of cellulose glue paint with a large paintbrush, using random criss-cross strokes. Allow each coat to dry for 6 hours before applying the next one.

For a semi-transparent colorwash, thin the paint.

Wash brushes and tools in warm, soapy water.

Cellulose glue paint is built up in several layers to produce a richly textured finish.

LIME WASH

Perfect for traditional buildings, the structures of which need to breathe in order to prevent dampness and other problems, lime wash is made from lime putty (i.e., calcium hydroxide, or slaked quicklime). Small amounts of additional ingredients, such as linseed oil, tallow, and casein, are sometimes added to the basic mix to improve its water-repellent properties. It has an attractive, soft matte finish.

SAFETY: Lime is a highly caustic alkali and must be handled with care. See detailed advice on page 41.

INGREDIENTS
2¼ pounds (1kg) lime putty

2 quarts (2 liters) water

7 ounces (200g) lime-tolerant natural pigment (about 1⅔ cups; see pages 36–39)

Only those pigments that can tolerate lime (mainly natural earths) should be used to color lime wash and lime paint (see recipe on page 64). The addition of pigments produces a range of beautiful pastel colors. Creams, yellows, pinks, apricots, and fawns can be made with combinations of red and yellow ochers, umbers, and siennas.

Using natural earth pigments enables the painter to experiment with tones and color combinations. Slight color variation is to be expected, and is actually one of the charms of lime mixtures, but try to keep a record of quantities used, and mix enough wash or paint to finish each coat in one try as duplicating exact color matches can be difficult.

The amounts given should cover 130 to 260 square feet (12 to 24 square meters).

Uses
Lime wash is suitable for interior and exterior use on absorbent surfaces. It is not washable.

Method
Slake the pigment (see page 36). For a paler, weaker color, use less than the full amount of pigment; do not exceed the given quantity.

Put the lime putty into a bucket, then gradually mix in the water using a whisk attachment on an electric beater. Sift the mixture into another bucket to remove any lumps or bits of grit. Add the slaked pigment and combine thoroughly with the drill whisk. Once mixed, this wash can be stored almost indefinitely in an airtight container.

Surfaces should be clean, free of grease and organic growth such as moss, lichen, etc. Remove loose or flaky material. Wet the substrate thoroughly to ease application and ensure that the lime wash does not dry too quickly, thereby preventing proper bonding. A pump-action garden spray is ideal for this purpose, but if you do not have one, use a large brush. Avoid application in strong wind or sunlight.

Application
Apply the watery wash really thinly with a long-haired masonry brush, working the brush in all directions. If it is applied too thickly or dries too quickly, the lime wash will craze and powder off when dry. The lime wash is translucent upon application but becomes opaque as it dries. The color also appears much lighter when dry than it does when wet.

Stir frequently during use. Let each coat dry for 24 to 48 hours, and redampen the wall with a spray or brush between coats. At least four coats are recommended; each coat adds to the lovely soft finish.

Wash brushes and tools in warm, soapy water.

The paint will appear dry and dusty for a few days until carbonation (the absorption of carbon dioxide from the atmosphere) has been completed, at which point the wall will effectively be coated with a thin layer of limestone.

Lime wash dries several shades lighter than the
wet paint. It is a good idea to paint a sample
board before painting the wall.

LIME PAINT

The binder in lime paint is hydraulic lime, which is supplied in powder form. It is produced from a form of limestone that contains some clay. When mixed with water, it becomes a paint (as distinct from lime wash, which is made from lime putty). Like lime wash, it has mild antiseptic and insect-repellent qualities and provides a vapor-permeable finish that lets buildings breathe, preventing problems such as dampness, condensation, and mold growth. One way in which it differs from lime wash is that fewer coats are required for a finish.

SAFETY: Lime is a highly caustic alkali and must be handled with care. See detailed advice on page 41.

INGREDIENTS
2¼ pounds (1kg) hydraulic lime

2 quarts (2 liters) water

3½ ounces (100g) lime-tolerant natural pigment (about ¾ cup; see advice on page 62)

The amounts given should cover approximately 130 to 260 square feet (12 to 24 square meters).

Uses
This paint is suitable for interior and exterior use on most porous surfaces, such as brick, stone, cement, and earth and gypsum plasters. It is not really washable.

Method
Making lime paint is not an exact science: Proportions given are a guideline only. You may need to thin the first coat for very absorbent surfaces.

Slake the pigment (see page 36). For a paler, weaker color, use less than the full amount of pigment; do not exceed the given quantity.

Place the lime in a bucket and gradually add the water, stirring continuously with a whisk attachment for an electric beater until the paint is thoroughly mixed and has an even consistency like light cream. Add the slaked pigment and combine it thoroughly with the paint.

This is only a short-lived paint because it reacts with water, so do not mix up more than you intend to use in one day.

Preparation
Surfaces should be clean, free of grease and organic growth such as moss, lichen, etc. Remove loose or flaky material. Wet the substrate thoroughly to ease application and ensure that the paint does not dry too quickly, thereby preventing proper bonding. A pump-action garden spray is ideal for this purpose, but if you do not have one, use a large brush.

Application
Apply the paint thinly and evenly with a long-haired masonry brush, using broad brush strokes. If applied too thickly, it will craze and

powder off when dry. The paint is translucent upon application but becomes opaque as it dries. The color also appears much lighter when dry than it does when wet. Stir the paint regularly during application. If there is some thick paint in the bottom of the bucket toward the end, stir in some more water to dilute it.

Apply two or three coats, wait 24 hours between coats. Redampen the wall with a spray or brush before applying the next coat.

Wash brushes and tools in warm, soapy water.

The paint will appear dry and dusty for a few days until carbonation (the absorption of carbon dioxide from the atmosphere) has been completed, at which point the wall will effectively be coated with a thin layer of limestone. If the paint dries too quickly, the carbonation process will not occur, so avoid application in strong wind or sunlight.

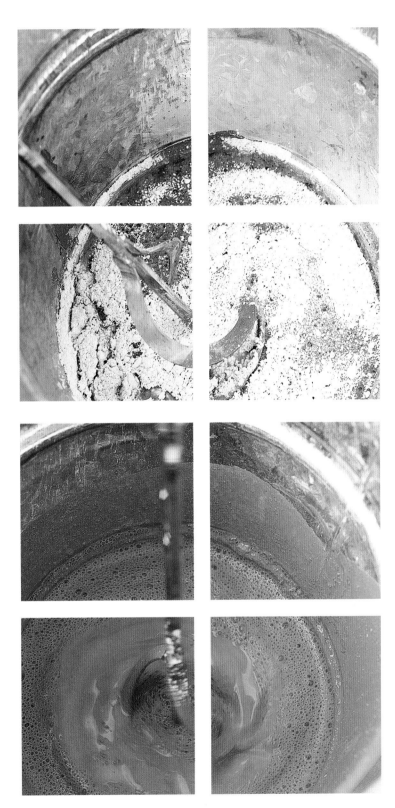

The natural colors of lime paint are a perfect foil
for an unusual wood and stone niche containing
an ancient key.

OIL PAINT

Natural oil paint takes a long time to dry. In fact, this linseed *oil–based* paint will never completely harden. The advantage of this is that it will remain elastic enough to move with the natural swelling and shrinking of the wood it is used to paint.

SAFETY: Avoid inhaling any kind of solvent. Work in a well-ventilated area. Wear a mask while sanding.

INGREDIENTS

Priming coat
½ cup (100ml) boiled linseed oil
½ cup (100ml) solvent (turpentine or citrus thinners)

First and second coats
½ cup (100ml) boiled linseed oil
3 tablespoons (20g) pigment
¼ cup (50ml) solvent

The pigment quantities used here are only a guideline—different types of pigment absorb very different amounts of oil.

The amounts given should cover approximately 16 to 22 square feet (1.5 to 2 square meters).

Uses
This paint is suitable for interior and exterior bare, unpainted wood. It is washable only after several weeks.

Preparation
Raise the grain of the wood by brushing some warm water onto it. Wipe the excess off after a few minutes with a lint-free cloth. Let the wood dry thoroughly before sanding it down.

Method
Make the priming coat by mixing the oil and solvent together in a bowl.

Make the paint by putting the pigment in a small bowl and adding enough linseed oil to blend it to a smooth paste. Gradually add the rest of the oil, and then the solvent.

Note that long drying times are needed between each coat.

Application
Brush the priming coat over the surface of the wood. After 10 minutes or so, remove any primer that has not been absorbed by wiping the surface with a lint-free cloth. Leave the area well ventilated overnight.

Apply the first coat very thinly, brushing it in the direction of the grain. If it is applied thickly, the paint will form a skin on the surface, preventing the rest of it from drying. Leave the area well ventilated for 48 hours.

Apply the second coat as for the first. Let it dry for several days.

Clean brushes and tools in some solvent.

Oil paint is a good choice for wooden surfaces because it remains elastic enough to expand and contract with the wood.

EGG AND OIL PAINT

In this recipe, egg is used not only as a binder but also as an emulsifier, meaning that the oil and water can be mixed and no solvent is needed. Choose darker pigments for exterior wood and paler ones for interior wood.

INGREDIENTS

1 egg

⅓ cup (80ml) boiled linseed oil

⅓ cup (80ml) water

**1 tablespoon natural pigment
(see pages 36–39)**

The amounts given should cover approximately 16 to 22 square feet (1.5 to 2 square meters).

Uses

This paint is suitable for interior and exterior bare, unpainted wood. It is washable after several weeks.

Method

Put the egg and oil in a bowl and whisk them together using an electric beater. Then very gradually whisk in the water. Put the pigment in another bowl and mix a little of this binder into it to make a smooth, lump-free paste. Gradually add the rest of the binder.

Brush the paint onto the wood using a medium paintbrush. For a less opaque finish, wait a few minutes and then wipe off any excess paint with an absorbent lint-free cloth to reveal the grain of the wood beneath. Otherwise, for a more opaque finish, use two or more coats of paint, letting each dry for about 48 hours between coats, keeping the area well ventilated.

This paint will take several days to dry thoroughly.

Wash brushes and tools in warm, soapy water.

Egg and oil paint produces an attractive finish
that emphasizes the natural grain of the wood.

TRANSPARENT OIL GLAZE

This basic recipe is very versatile and adaptable. It can be used to make casein powder and borax paint on walls and woodwork more dirt resistant and strong enough to be wiped clean. It can also add a layer of subtle color to walls or be used to stain internal and external bare wood. Finally, if you omit the pigment, the oil alone will darken the color of casein powder and borax paint.

SAFETY: Avoid inhaling any kind of solvent. Work in a well-ventilated area.

INGREDIENTS
½ cup (100ml) boiled linseed oil

⅓ cup (80ml) solvent (turpentine or citrus thinners)

1 tablespoon whiting

½ teaspoon natural pigment (see pages 36–39)

The amounts given should cover approximately 27 square feet (2.5 square meters).

Method
Put a little of your chosen solvent in a bowl, then dissolve some or all of the pigment and whiting in it (the amount depends on the desired effect and the type of pigment and whiting).

Mix the rest of the thinner with the linseed oil in another bowl, and then add the dissolved pigment.

Application
Apply one coat, using a colorwash brush for walls or a medium paintbrush for woodwork. Note that linseed oil will take several days to dry thoroughly.

Clean brushes and tools in some solvent and then wash in warm, soapy water.

Here, transparent oil glaze has been used to add
a subtle layer of color to a bare wood floor.

STAINING WOOD WITH PLANT COLOR

Plant dyes have a translucent quality because light can pass through the molecules of color (whereas it is reflected off the grains of a natural pigment). Any plant that leaves a stain on your hands can probably be used to make a basic dye; simply boil the plant material in water to extract the color. Different plants will naturally produce different colors; for example, onion skins make a yellow dye, beets a deep red to pink, and blackberries a purple-pink. Be aware that plant dyes are not light-fast and will fade over time.

INGREDIENTS
Plant material
Water

Method
Put the plant material in a saucepan and just cover it with water. Boil, and then let it steep. The more material boiled and the longer it is steeped, the darker the dye will be. Strain the cooled mixture into a bowl through a colander or strainer lined with muslin or cheesecloth.

Application
Apply the stain to the wood with a medium paintbrush or lint-free cloth. Let it dry thoroughly before sanding the surface lightly. Add another coat, if necessary, then protect the surface with oil or wax.
Wash brushes and tools in warm, soapy water.

From left to right: Frames stained with beets, saffron, tea and iron acetate, cochineal, and onion skins.

STAINING WOOD WITH TEA AND VINEGAR

Tannins are naturally present in woods like oak, but pale woods like pine can be darkened by having tannins added to them in the form of strong black tea. Iron acetate, when applied to the wood, reacts with tannins to produce a rich, dark color.

Like the transparent oil glaze (page 72), this recipe is open to a lot of experimentation. The results can be unpredictable, so conduct some trials first before applying either of the two stains to your woodwork.

INGREDIENTS

To add tannins:
2¼ cups (500ml) water
⅛ cup (25g) Indian tea leaves

For iron acetate:
Large ball of fine steel wool
Malt vinegar

Method

For the tannin mixture, boil the water and add it to the tea leaves. Let the tea steep for an hour or two, then strain it into a bowl.

For the iron acetate mixture, place the steel wool in a jar and cover it with the malt vinegar. Screw the lid on and leave it overnight. The next day, strain the mixture through a colander or strainer lined with muslin or cheesecloth to remove all the steel wool. (For a more powerful iron acetate solution, use more steel wool, or let it soak longer.)

Application

Apply the tannin mixture to the wood with a medium paintbrush or lint-free cloth. Leave it for a few minutes before wiping off any excess with a lint-free cloth. Some pale woods will be colored by this process alone. Let it dry.

Now apply the iron acetate solution to the wood with a medium paintbrush or lint-free cloth. The wood should start to darken immediately and can continue to darken for up to half an hour.

Let the wood dry thoroughly before sanding it lightly. You can then apply an oil or wax finish.

Wash brushes and tools in warm, soapy water.

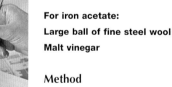

Experiment with painted sample boards to achieve the finish you want.

FLOOR AND FURNITURE WAX

In this basic floor and furniture wax, beeswax is mixed with a solvent to form a soft paste. The addition of other types of wax will change the quality of the finish; carnauba, for example, will make it harder.

SAFETY: Avoid inhaling any kind of solvents.

INGREDIENTS
2 ounces (50g) beeswax
½ cup (100ml) solvent (turpentine or citrus thinners)

Method
Put the beeswax into a wide jar. Stand the jar in a saucepan of hot water and heat it very gently until the wax has melted. Wax is a flammable material, so be very careful not to overheat it.

Remove the jar from the saucepan, stir in the solvent, and let the mixture cool to a wax paste.

Application
Apply the wax to the floor or piece of furniture with a soft, lint-free cloth, and buff to a soft sheen.

Clean brushes and tools in some solvent and then wash in warm, soapy water. Wash the waxing cloth in hot water and detergent.

Natural floor and furniture wax can be used
on any wooden surface, from picture frames
to wooden floors.

LIMING WAX

This recipe adds color to the floor and furniture wax (see page 78), or it can be added to a store-bought beeswax furniture wax if you prefer not to make your own. Liming wax is traditionally white and is used to highlight the grain of bare wood, but this should by no means be its limit. Try experimenting with different colors and using it not only on bare wood but also over casein powder and borax paint or on plaster moldings.

INGREDIENTS
3½ ounces (100g) beeswax-based
    furniture wax (about ½ cup)
1½ ounces (30g) natural pigment
    (about ⅓ cup; see pages 36–39)

Method
Thoroughly combine the two ingredients in a small dish using a palette knife or butter knife.

Application
Apply the wax paste to your surface using fine steel wool or a soft, lint-free cloth. Push the wax into the pores, cracks, and moldings. Buff the wax with a pan scourer or shoe brush to give a soft, water-repellent, protective sheen.

Clean brushes and tools in warm, soapy water.

The application of blue pigment to the basic furniture wax results in a more complex finish.

BEER GLAZE

The binder in this glaze is the starch and sugar of lager beer. As a binder for pigment, lager is transparent, viscous, and slow-drying—qualities that make it ideal for use as a colorwash for a pure reflection of light from the natural colored pigments.

INGREDIENTS

1 quart (1 liter) lager beer

1 tablespoon natural pigment (see pages 36–39)

The amounts given should cover approximately 430 square feet (40 square meters).

Uses

This glaze is suitable for absorbent walls. It is not washable, so use it to decorate very low-wear surfaces, such as ceilings.

Method

Slake the pigment (see page 36). Mix the beer and the slaked pigment together in a bowl.

Application

This glaze will dry in 1 to 2 hours and can be washed off during the drying time, so you will have plenty of time to experiment with different combinations of color and texture. Wash brushes and tools in warm, soapy water.

The light-reflecting properties of beer glaze
are the perfect counterpoint to the delicacy of
white blossoms.

GLAIR PAINT

Egg white was historically used as a binder to make paints for illuminated manuscripts.

INGREDIENTS
1 egg white

**½ teaspoon natural pigment
(see pages 36–39)**

The amounts given will cover approximately 10 to 16 square feet (1 to 1.5 square meters).

Uses
This delicate transparent paint is suitable for hand-painted details on absorbent surfaces. It is not washable.

Method
Slake the pigment (see page 36). Put the egg white in a small bowl and gently whisk it to a slight froth. Let stand until the clear liquid glair separates away from the froth, then remove the froth with a metal spoon. Gradually mix your chosen pigment into the remaining glair using an artist's paintbrush. Be careful not to add too much—the idea is to aim for a very delicate, transparent finish.

Application
Apply the paint using the artist's paintbrush. Leave it to dry for approximately 30 minutes.

Wash brushes and tools in warm, soapy water.

A plain lamp shade is transformed by the application of glair paint.

WATER-BASED PAINT

Gum arabic is a resin exuded by several species of acacia trees. The resulting tears are crushed up and then dissolved in water to form a gum solution. Gum arabic has traditionally been used as a binder for two artists' paints: watercolor and gouache. Whether you end up with a really transparent paint or something more opaque depends on the type and quantity of pigment used (see page 36). The honey is added to keep the paint flexible.

INGREDIENTS

**1 ounce (25g) gum arabic (about 2
    tablespoons)**

½ cup (100ml) water

2 teaspoons (10g) honey

**1 tablespoon natural pigment
    (see pages 36–39)**

Uses
This paint is suitable for hand-painted details on absorbent surfaces. It is not washable.

Method
Grind up the tears of gum arabic as finely as possible in a mortar and pestle. Put the water in the top of a double boiler, add the gum arabic, and heat the mixture gently until the gum has dissolved. Add the honey, then remove the pan from the heat and let the mixture cool.

Put your chosen pigment in a small bowl and add a little of the binder, blending it to a smooth, lump-free paste. Gradually add the rest of the binder.

Application
Use a soft artist's paintbrush to apply this paint, leaving half an hour between coats.

Wash brushes and tools in warm, soapy water.

Water-based paints such as this one are suitable for adding the finishing touches to a wall.

EGG TEMPERA

Egg yolk was historically used as a binder in icon painting. The results are a rich paint best suited to small-scale decorative projects. Just like dried egg yolk on a plate, this paint will not rub off, but it can be scratched away.

The quantity of pigment needed varies according to type (see pages 36–39). A great metallic paint can be achieved by mixing "glimmer" pigments with the yolk.

INGREDIENTS
1 egg yolk

½ teaspoon natural pigment (see pages 36–39)

Uses
Suitable for stenciling and decorative free-hand painting on absorbent surfaces. It can be wiped clean but is not washable.

Method
Gently place the egg yolk on a saucer lined with a piece of paper towel. Leave it for about 5 minutes to dry slightly so that you can gently pick it up. Place it in a shallow bowl and remove the sac by pinching it between the very tips of your forefinger and thumb, while carefully piercing it with the tip of an artist's paintbrush. The contents should run out easily.

Gradually add some pigment to the yolk, mixing it in with your brush. Do not add all the pigment at once because too much will result in a dry and flaky paint rather than a rich one.

Application
Apply the egg tempera with a soft artist's paintbrush. Or, using a sponge or stencil brush for stenciling, work fairly quickly so that the mixture does not start to dry and form a skin. Add a little water if necessary. One coat should be enough.

Wash brushes and tools in warm, soapy water before the paint dries.

The tempera will be dry to the touch in 1 hour and will continue to harden over a few days.

Egg tempera can be used to great effect on
small-scale decorative objects such as
this lamp base.

GESSO

Gesso was traditionally used to coat carved softwood furniture, building up a hard finish that not only smoothed over rough and imperfect wood and joinery but also provided a porcelain-smooth base for subsequent gilding or painting.

SAFETY: Always wear a mask when sanding.

INGREDIENTS
2 ounces (50g) rabbit-skin glue granules (about ¼ cup)
2¼ cups (500ml) warm water
18 ounces (500g) prepared whiting (see page 36)

Method
Put the water in the top part of a double boiler, heat until warm, then add the glue granules. When the granules have dissolved, turn off the heat and leave the mixture in the pan overnight. In the morning, the solution will have set, but gentle heating will melt it again. Be careful not to overheat the glue. Use a little of this glue to prime the wood before continuing with the recipe.

Remove the saucepan from the heat and gradually sift the whiting into the remaining glue, stirring it thoroughly to make a creamy paint. Add more water if the mixture seems too thick. Test a little of the cooling mixture between your thumb and forefinger—it will become tacky as it starts to set.

This basic mix can be tinted with slaked natural pigments (see pages 36–39), if desired.

Application
Apply the gesso while it is still warm and fluid. You will need to apply several coats with a flat brush. Let each coat dry before applying the next, and sand lightly between coats. You will need to reheat the mixture gently for each coat since it sets as it cools.

As the coats build up, the drying time will increase from a few minutes to a couple of hours for the final coat. Brushing at right angles to the previous coat will help to build up a thick finish.

When the final coat is completely dry, sand the gesso to a superfine surface with fine steel wool or sandpaper. Burnish the finish with a soft cloth and a little wax polish.

Wash brushes and tools in warm, soapy water.

Gesso provides a smooth finish for painted wooden objects, such as this small decorative shelf.

This page, top to bottom:
A paneled door made beautiful by marbling, an attic bedroom painted in a warm earth tone, china objects against a beautiful wall, and a terra-cotta wall transformed by light and shadow.
Opposite: Walls and furnishings are blended through thoughtful use of color and texture.

With a little imagination, natural paints can be
used to create myriad decorative effects

CREATIVE DECORATIVE TECHNIQUES AND EFFECTS

The aim of this chapter is to outline some basic ways in which the paint recipes from the previous chapter, together with specially formulated commercial products, can be applied in order to make the most of their particular properties. A list of suppliers and recommendations on how to choose ready-made natural paints that are suited to your specific requirements can be found in the appendix (pages 182 to 184). We hope to demonstrate that very few materials are needed in order to create a wide variety of effects, and that creativity and imagination are sometimes the most important ingredients.

WALLS AND DETAILING

Ironically, some standard decorative paint techniques have the goal of reproducing the subtle variations in tone and texture that will come quite naturally when you are using ecopaints or mixing your own paint. Furthermore, just by using paints that have been colored with natural earth and mineral pigments—either those you have tinted yourself (see page 164) or ready-colored natural emulsions—you will discover a subtle depth and variation in tone. This is due to the fact that the natural pigments have a crystalline structure and reflect light from the surface of the paint in numerous directions. This quality can only really be appreciated by witnessing it in real life, but the examples shown in this book demonstrate that extremely pleasing results can easily be obtained without employing any special techniques. However, since some of us are unable to resist the urge to experiment, here are some basic decorative techniques that have the potential for very subtle or quite dramatic results.

ROLLER FIDGETING

The aim of this simple technique is to blend two colors together in a random fashion across a wall. For a harmonious, understated effect, choose two colors that are fairly similar (close together on the color wheel; see page 164), or even two shades of the same color. Contrasting colors can give more dramatic results, but it might be wise to keep this effect to a restricted area, such as a chimney breast or around the headboard of a bed in an otherwise plain room.

Materials
Ecopaint in two different colors

Equipment
Roller tray
Long-pile roller
Small paintbrush

Preparation
The wall to be painted should be clean and sound.

Method
You could either use two ecopaints that have already been colored by the manufacturer or tint some white ecopaint yourself. Mix slaked natural pigments (see page 36) into two different cans of the base paint. You might want to experiment with quantities until you achieve the depth of color you want.

Application

Pour equal amounts of each color into a roller tray, one on each side. Roll a long-pile roller across the tray so that each half of the roller is coated with a different color. Apply the paint to the wall using short, gentle strokes in different directions.

The more you work over the surface of the wall, the more blended the colors will become. Stand back to view your results regularly. Use a small paintbrush to stipple color into the corners.

Roller fidgeting produces a subtle textured result on a plain wall.

SHADING

Mixing your own pigment into a ready-made ecopaint is a great way of maximizing the fact that you have control over color and depth of shade. The possibilities are as varied as your imagination, so, before you start mixing and painting, spend some time thinking about the effect you want to achieve. It is worth sketching out a few ideas on some scrap paper first and then marking out points on the wall where you intend to change to another color or shade, so that you can visualize the end result and how it might alter the look of the room.

Materials
White ecopaint
Natural pigments

Equipment
4-inch (10cm) paintbrush or
Medium-pile roller and tray
Sponge

Preparation
The wall to be painted should be clean and sound.

Method
Tint all the paint with a small amount of slaked natural pigment (see page 36). During the application, you will be adding more pigment.

APPLICATION FOR MONOCHROME SHADING
Paint an area of wall with the tinted paint using a paintbrush or medium-pile roller, whichever you prefer. Now add a little more pigment to the remaining paint and paint the area immediately adjacent to the first, overlapping a little and blending the transition with a slightly dampened sponge. Keep working around the room, adding small amounts of pigment as you go. You might find it easier to do this with a partner, especially if you are covering a large area.

Or, begin by painting the ceiling in a very pale shade of your chosen color, then gradually work down the walls, adding more pigment as you go, until by the time you reach the baseboard the paint is a deep shade of the original color. This particular example would have the effect of making the ceiling appear higher, but it could be reversed for the opposite effect.

Rather than tackling a whole room, a simple idea is to add more pigment to the paint in just one area around a feature of the room, such as a fireplace, door, or window. The effect could be kept soft and only just noticeable, or made into a really striking feature.

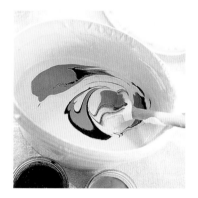

APPLICATION FOR
MULTICOLOR SHADING

Follow the technique for monochrome shading, but add different pigments as you go, so that as you work around the room you gradually move from one color to another, and another. This might work really well in an open-plan living space to demarcate but connect different areas and create different moods. Imagine a deep red fireplace gradually mellowing out to a warm ocher living room.

Shading adds an extra dimension of interest to an alcove containing a wood-burning stove.

COLORWASHING

Colorwashing is a very versatile technique. The idea is simply to add layers of color to a wall, but the finished effect will vary greatly according to the medium and color used, rate of dilution, number of layers, and method of application. It is advisable to paint a series of sample boards (see page 39) or practice on a wall that can be repainted easily so that you can get a feel for the performance and resulting effects of your chosen materials. Do not feel limited to the suggested applications outlined here, but rather see them as a starting point for experimentation and the development of your own ideas.

Colorwashing can be an economical method of making a little colored pigment go a long way. It also makes a good base for stenciling and hand-painted decorative details. There are two basic types of colorwash: semitransparent and transparent. Semitransparent colorwashes are usually thinned latex paint or casein paint, which will dry fairly quickly, resulting in a flat finish. Transparent colorwashes will give more depth to the finish and will either include some oil in the recipe, thereby having a longer drying time, or be based on a binder plus colored pigment, but no filler.

PAINT IT WHITE

On moving into a new home, many people will just paint the whole interior with white paint. This serves two purposes: First, it means that they don't have to think about choosing colors at a time when life is hectic enough already, and second, it provides a clean start and a blank canvas to which color can be added later.

A white base is particularly suitable for a colorwash technique because light is reflected back from it, through the thin colored layer; but colored bases can also be colorwashed. Choose a white ecopaint and apply it with a brush rather than a roller, so that you can create a nicely brush-textured background that will be highlighted by a colorwash later. This approach is ideal if you want to decorate with natural products, and especially if you want to use some of the colorwash recipes from chapter 3.

Sample boards show a range of effects that can be produced using colorwashing.

COLORWASH

This is an outline of the basic technique. You will need to apply at least two layers of color for a good effect.

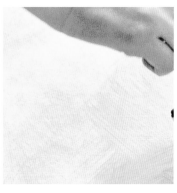

Materials

Colorwash—transparent or semi-transparent

Equipment

Wide paintbrush, colorwash brush, or large bath sponge

Paintbrush, softening brush, or cloth to mop up runs and soften or create texture

Preparation

The wall to be painted should be clean and sound. Apply two coats of white ecopaint as a base for the colorwash.

Application

Apply a thin layer of colorwash to the entire chosen area, either using broad, sweeping brushstrokes or literally washing it on with a large bath sponge. Work quickly to cover the whole area from one side to the other, softening hard edges as you go and before they dry. Don't worry about missing patches or any unevenness of color at this stage.

Avoid overloading the brush or sponge to prevent the wash from running down the wall, and keep a dry brush or cloth handy to mop up any runs that do occur. Step back to view your work regularly.

Allow the first layer to dry thoroughly before repeating the process, this time covering the parts you missed before, plus some of the first layer of wash. Further layers will deepen the color. Let each layer dry thoroughly before applying the next.

There are many ways to vary this basic technique, and it really is a good idea to practice first. You could soften the brush or sponge marks by working over the still wet colorwash with a dry softening brush; it might help to have a partner working with you for this part. Otherwise, you could remove areas of color by working carefully with a very slightly damp brush or sponge.

A transparent colorwash will dry more slowly than a thinned paint, giving you more time to soften brushstrokes and create texture. A thicker, semitransparent wash applied with a brush will leave a more obvious texture than a thin one applied with a sponge.

Applying successive layers of colorwash
produces a subtle, graded effect.

SHADING WITH A SEMITRANSPARENT COLORWASH

This is a very simple way of controlling the slow buildup of color in a room.

Materials
Colorwash made from thinned casein or latex paint

Equipment
Wide paintbrush, colorwash brush, or large bath sponge
Paintbrush, softening brush, or cloth to mop up runs

Preparation
The wall to be painted should be clean and sound. Apply two coats of white ecopaint as a base for the colorwash.

Application
Apply a thin layer of colorwash to the entire chosen area, either using broad, sweeping brushstrokes or literally washing it on with a large bath sponge. Work quickly to cover the whole area from one side to the other, softening hard edges as you go and before they dry. Don't worry about missing patches or any unevenness of color at this stage.

Avoid overloading the brush or sponge to prevent the wash from running down the wall, and keep a dry brush or cloth handy to mop up any runs that do occur. Step back to view your work regularly.

Let the first layer dry before repeating the same process, but this time wash only four-fifths of the way up the wall. Keep repeating layers, covering three-fifths, then two-fifths, and finally just one-fifth of the wall. Each successive layer of wash will leave more depth of color, so the room will be colored more strongly at the bottom than at the top. Let each layer dry thoroughly before applying the next.

See Shading (page 98) for more inspiration on ways to use this technique.

The technique of building up layers of semi-transparent wash means that the color can be as vivid or as subdued as you want to make it.

LAYERING COLOR WITH A TRANSPARENT COLORWASH

The qualities of a transparent wash will let each layer of color show through successive layers, and subsequent coats will alter the color of those that have preceded them. Yellow washed over pink, for example, will result in an apricot color. Consult the color wheel on page 164 to see which colors are produced by the combination of two others. Don't feel that you have to cover every wall with every color—particular combinations can be confined to individual areas.

Materials
A selection of transparent colorwashes

Equipment
Wide brush, colorwash brush, or large bath sponge
Paintbrush, softening brush, or cloth to mop up runs and soften or create texture

Preparation
The wall to be painted should be clean and sound. Apply two coats of white ecopaint as a base for the colorwash.

Think carefully about which colors you want to combine, and in which order. Generally speaking, layer paler colors over darker ones, and keep color combinations simple to avoid ending up with a muddy effect. It would be a good idea to paint some sample boards (see page 39).

Application
Apply a thin layer of colorwash to the entire chosen area, either using broad, sweeping brushstrokes or literally washing it on with a large bath sponge. Work quickly to cover the whole area from one side to the other, softening hard edges as you go and before they dry. Don't worry about missing patches or any unevenness of color at this stage.

Avoid overloading the brush or sponge to prevent the wash from running down the wall, and keep a dry brush or cloth handy to mop up any runs that do occur. Step back to view your work regularly.

Let the first layer dry thoroughly before adding a different colorwash. A transparent wash containing oil will dry more slowly than a thinned latex paint or casein paint, so you will have more time to soften brushstrokes or create texture. Let each layer dry thoroughly before applying the next.

Transparent colorwashes let you mix and match
colors according to your imagination.

SPONGING OR RAGGING ON

This is another basically simple technique that can result in a wide variety of textured effects, depending on the type of colorwash, combination of colors, and material used to apply it. Choose from a natural sponge, synthetic sponge with lumps pulled out of it to create texture, or some kind of fabric, such as cotton cloth, chamois leather, cheesecloth, or burlap.

Materials
Colorwash—transparent or
  semitransparent, in one or more
  colors

Equipment
Sponge or fabric

Preparation
The wall to be painted should be clean and sound. Apply two coats of white ecopaint as a base for the colorwash.

Application
Dip the sponge or fabric into the colorwash and squeeze out the excess liquid. If using fabric, scrunch it into a loose ball. Dab the sponge or fabric onto newspaper, cardboard, or something similar to test the effect. Repeat this sequence each time you reload the sponge or fabric ball with wash, rather than just applying it straight onto the wall.

Dab the sponge or fabric ball gently onto the wall to leave textured marks. Work quickly and randomly over the whole area.

Don't worry about gaps; subsequent layers of wash will fill these as well as overlapping the first layer in places.

Let each layer dry thoroughly before applying the next. You can experiment with combinations of two or more colors, or with two shades of the same color. Begin by applying the darkest first.

For a different texture, try dipping a cloth into the colorwash, squeezing it out, and then twisting it into a loose sausage shape, which you can then roll across the wall in random directions.

The type and shape of the material used for sponging or ragging on can be varied depending on the effect you wish to achieve.

CREATING TEXTURE WITH A ROLLER

It is best to work with a partner for this technique, with one person applying the glaze/wash and the other following behind, using an adapted foam roller to pull the glaze/wash randomly into an irregular pattern before it dries.

Materials
Color concentrates or pigments
Glazing or colorwash medium

Equipment
Long-haired brushes
**Standard foam roller with holes
  plucked out of the foam**

Preparation
The wall to be painted should be clean and sound. Apply two coats of white or colored ecopaint as a base for the glaze/wash.

Method
Make up two glazes/washes according to the manufacturer's instructions; for example, one umber and one yellow ocher. If

you are nervous about achieving the effect you want, simply dilute the glazes/washes further so that the pigmentation is less intense.

Application
Dip the brush first into one glaze/wash and then into the other. Brush the mixture onto the wall in a loose, criss-cross fashion. This technique results in differing amounts of each color being picked up each time, giving a subtle variation in color—sometimes more brown, sometimes more yellow—and an overall honey shade.

Work over the whole area quickly from one side to the other, trying not to let hard edges dry.

Try not to be afraid of making mistakes.

Work over the entire area several times until you have built up the strength of color you want, but let each layer dry thoroughly before adding the next.

Using this technique in a newly renovated barn creates a feeling of intimacy and warmth in an otherwise unwelcoming interior.

STIPPLING

Use a dry stippling brush, or any brush with short, rigid bristles, to create this simple but effective texture.

Materials
Color concentrates or pigments
Glazing or colorwash medium

Equipment
Long-haired brush
Stippling brush

Preparation
The wall to be painted should be clean and sound. Apply two coats of white or colored ecopaint as a base for the glaze/wash.

Method
Make up a glaze/wash according to the manufacturer's instructions.

Application
Apply the glaze/wash using loose brushstrokes. You could use one color or more (see page 110). Gently stipple out the obvious brushstrokes as you go, using the same brush.

It is best to work with a partner, one applying the glaze/wash and the other following behind. Use the dry stippling brush while the

color is still wet to "pounce" firmly onto the surface, revealing the base coat in a subtle texture of small dots. Clean the stippling brush on waste paper when it begins to become loaded with glaze/wash—the aim is to remove color rather than add more.

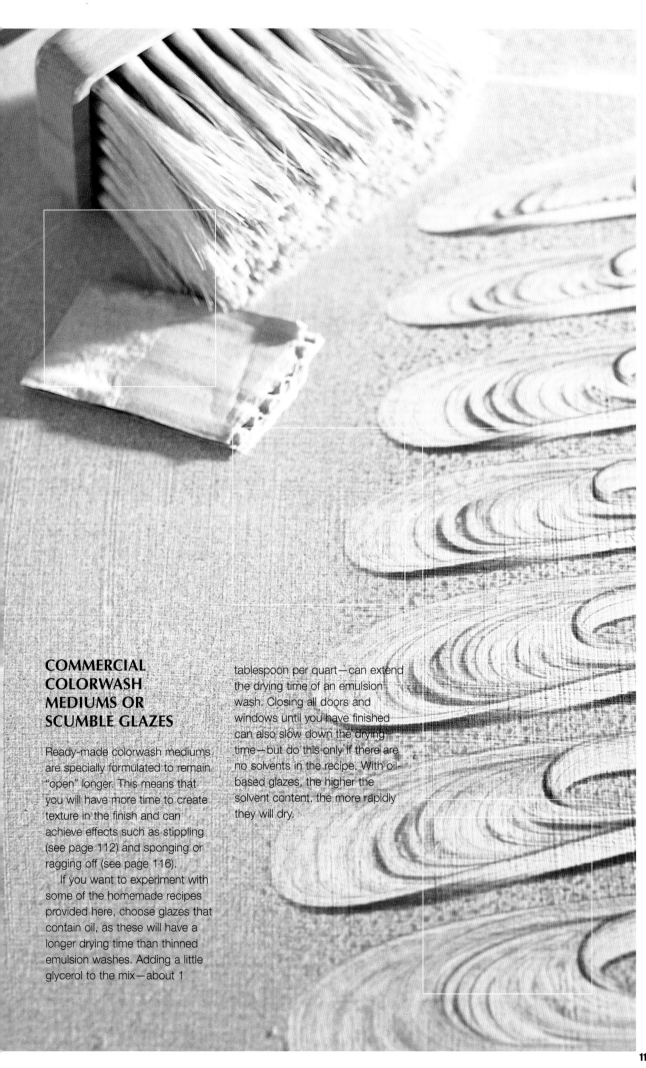

COMMERCIAL COLORWASH MEDIUMS OR SCUMBLE GLAZES

Ready-made colorwash mediums are specially formulated to remain "open" longer. This means that you will have more time to create texture in the finish and can achieve effects such as stippling (see page 112) and sponging or ragging off (see page 116).

If you want to experiment with some of the homemade recipes provided here, choose glazes that contain oil, as these will have a longer drying time than thinned emulsion washes. Adding a little glycerol to the mix—about 1 tablespoon per quart—can extend the drying time of an emulsion wash. Closing all doors and windows until you have finished can also slow down the drying time—but do this only if there are no solvents in the recipe. With oil-based glazes, the higher the solvent content, the more rapidly they will dry.

DRAGGING AND COMBING

A variation on stippling (see page 112) is to prepare the base and apply the glaze/colorwash in the same way as for stippling, but then reveal the base color by passing a long-haired brush or a comb through the wet glaze/wash. Successful straight dragging over a large area is difficult to master, but interesting, even wavy lines combed through the color can be effective. Consider using a glaze/wash that contrasts markedly with the base color by choosing two colors that appear far apart on the color wheel (see page 164).

SPONGING OR RAGGING OFF

These techniques are similar to stippling (see page 112) and dragging and combing (see page 114), but instead of *applying* textured color with a sponge or rag, they create texture by *removing* glaze or colorwash to reveal the base color.

Materials
Color concentrates or pigments
Glazing or colorwash medium

Equipment
Long-haired brush
**Natural sponge or lint-free fabric
    such as cotton, chamois leather,
    cheesecloth, or burlap**

Preparation
The wall to be painted should be clean and sound. Apply two coats of white or colored ecopaint as a base for the glaze/wash.

Method
Make up a glaze/colorwash according to the manufacturer's instructions.

Application
Brush the glaze/wash onto the wall using broad movements. Soften the brush marks by immediately stippling the glaze/wash with the same brush.
    While the glaze/wash is still wet, remove some of it by dabbing with a sponge or a scrunched-up piece of fabric. Wash the sponge out or use a fresh cloth regularly to avoid a buildup of glaze/wash.

    Work over the whole area fairly quickly before the glaze/wash dries to form hard edges. It is best to work with a partner, one applying the glaze/wash and the other following behind. If you work alone, work on small areas of about 1 square yard (1 square meter) at a time, always ensuring that the hard edges do not dry out to leave dark patches where thick color has overlapped a section.

Stippling creates an interestingly textured
surface, suitable for many areas of the house.

RAG ROLLING, FROTTAGE, AND BAGGING

These are variations on the theme of sponging or ragging off (see page 116), but they achieve different effects and textures by removing the glaze or colorwash using various materials and techniques. For example, try twisting a piece of fabric into a loose sausage shape and rolling it up the wall, changing the cloth frequently. Alternatively, experiment by removing glaze with sheets of newspaper, tissue paper, or scrunched-up plastic bags.

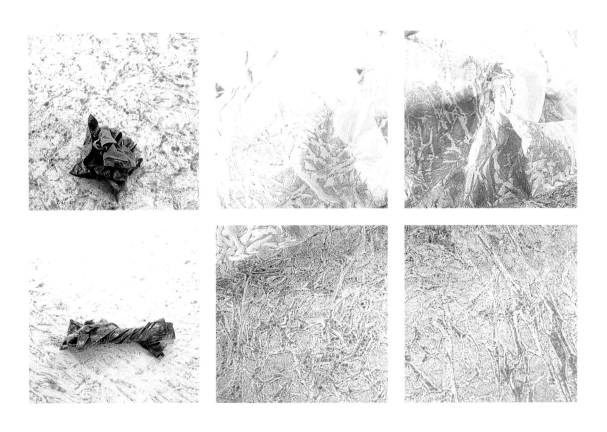

You can experiment with many different materials
to produce interesting and unusual effects.

STENCILING

Stenciling is an inexpensive way of adding decorative detail. Once the principles are mastered, the possibilities for creative application are enormous. The recipe for egg tempera on page 88 is ideal for stenciling. Inspiration for your own design is as close as fabric or other decorative details already in the room. It is generally best to keep designs simple.

Materials
Paint or glaze

Equipment
Plumb line
Tape measure
Level
Precut stencil, oiled card, or acetate
Utility knife
Low-tack masking tape
Stencil brush or small, firm sponge

Preparation
The wall to be painted should be clean and sound. Apply two coats of white or colored ecopaint as a base for the stenciling. If you are creating a border or a regularly repeating pattern, mark the position of the designs on the wall. Use a plumb line, tape measure, and level to be accurate.

Method
If you are making your own stencil, draw your design onto a piece of oiled card or acetate, and cut it out using a utility knife.

Application
Hold the stencil in position by hand or with the help of some low-tack masking tape. Make sure that your paint is not too runny to avoid it seeping under the edge of the stencil. Load your brush or sponge with only a very small amount of paint, and remove any excess by dabbing it onto some cloth or newspaper first.

Starting at the edges of the design and working inward, carefully apply your chosen paint or glaze by dabbing the stencil with the brush or sponge. Hold the stencil in place for a few moments afterward to let it dry slightly. Clean the stencil regularly to avoid a buildup of paint around the cutout design.

Simple graphic designs are the best choice when deciding upon a stencil template.

REVERSE STENCILING

Cut out a solid shape from card or acetate and use it as a mask while you apply more paint or glaze to the surrounding area. Once the mask is removed, the original base color will remain in that shape.

WAX RESIST

A variation of reverse stenciling is to create a wax-resist design on a wall by stenciling the design with soft furniture wax instead of paint. The wax will then resist any subsequent application of a colorwash over the whole area and can be carefully removed, leaving the design in the original base color.

 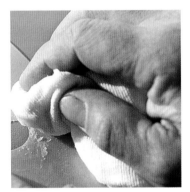

STENCILING WITH OIL GLAZE OR WAX

Oil glaze and furniture wax are particularly suitable for stenciling onto a base of casein paint because the design will simply be left in a darker shade of the original color.

DISTRESSED STENCILING

Once dry, stenciled images can be lightly sandpapered to soften or "age" them.

FREEHAND PAINTING

Several of the paint recipes from the previous chapter can be employed to create hand-painted decorative details on interior walls. Use light pencil marks, charcoal, or chalk to trace the outline of intricate designs or calligraphy onto the wall before filling them in with paint.

Even those of us who are not confident enough to create complicated images or a full-blown mural can add completely individual decoration to our interiors. The recipe for glair paint, for example (page 84), or a simple semitransparent colorwash such as the one based on quark (page 48) could be used to create soft swirls of color and subtle suggestions of movement. Apply with a large, soft, artists' quality or colorwash brush. Hand-painted or stenciled detail can then be added to this background.

On the other hand, the addition of freehand painted detail can lift a repetitive stenciled design into another dimension. The recipe for water-based paint (page 86) would be ideal for creating a faux 'shadow' along one side of a stenciled image. Use an artists' quality lining brush to apply the detail. The recipe for egg tempera (page 88) could be used to add some small spots of a contrasting color or to apply glimmer pigments as a highlight.

A steady hand is needed for freehand painting.

SOFTENED GLAZEWORK

A whole design can be pulled together, and stencils blended into the background, by the application of a thin wash of paint or glaze over the surface. The glaze can be tinted with a little pigment—raw or burnt umber is often used to tone down colors and give a warmer, aged look to a design.

An oil glaze will give an added richness and depth to the surface of a wall. You could experiment with the quark and oil glaze (page 50) or transparent oil glaze (page 72). The linseed oil content of either of these finishes will take a couple of weeks to dry properly. If applied over casein paint, they will render it temporarily transparent. For a faster-drying finish, use a brand-name glaze medium (see appendix page 182).

All of the above glazes will result in a darker color to the underlying paint, and give it a slight sheen. They will also make the surface easier to wipe and dirt-resistant—this functional quality can be applied in a creative way by, for example, laying on an oil glaze to chair height in the hallway or to 'children's finger' height up the stairs. If there is no actual chair rail you could demarcate your own line with creative masking.

For a matte, but non-wipable finish, try a thinned version of cellulose glue paint (page 60) omitting the whiting. The beer glaze (page 82) would also be ideal, in certain situations, to soften a stenciled design.

Applying a glaze over the top of a stenciled
design gives a coherence to the scheme.

WOODWORK AND FLOORING

Wood is rightly valued as a flooring material for its beauty, strength, and flexibility. There are some good reasons, both practical and aesthetic, why this natural material benefits from treatment with natural products rather than synthetic alternatives such as polyurethane varnish.

Wood was once a living tree. It has pores through which it will continue to regulate its moisture content by means of vapor exchange with the surrounding environment. Why seal lumber with a plastic film in an effort to prevent it from behaving like the natural material it is, when microporous oils and waxes will both protect the floor and let the wood continue to breathe?

NATURAL AROMATIC OIL FINISH

Filling the wood pores with natural oil means that there is less room for moisture to enter the wood, thereby regulating the swelling and shrinking of the floorboards. If the wood does move, the finish moves with it. If any moisture does enter, it will not be prevented from leaving by a hard, impermeable layer of synthetic varnish but will safely diffuse through the microporous finish.

Natural oils are very similar to those that a growing tree uses to protect and nourish itself. Plant oil is ideal for the impregnation of wood because its molecular structure is far finer than that of synthetic resins. Linseed oil molecules, for example, are ten times smaller than the narrowest passages in the cellular structure of wood. This means that the oil can penetrate especially deeply to merge with the resins already in the wood.

Deep impregnation and good bonding mean long-term performance. This finish is not going to scratch or chip off because it is, after all, now a part of the structure of the wood. It can also be easily spot-repaired and replenished: Just clean it up and apply more oil or wax. Plastic finishes, by contrast, are notoriously hard to touch up because the overlaps always show, they don't bond chemically to previous layers, and polyurethane also loses gloss with heavy wear, so the new patch will be too shiny. This can ultimately mean resanding the floor and starting again.

On a personal level, treating your floor with plant-based products is treating yourself to a sensory experience. Applying oil to bare wood can be an altogether nourishing process as you witness how the color and grain of the wood are marvelously accentuated. A few drops of some exotically scented wood oils, such as juniper, sandalwood, or amyris essential oils, could even be

incorporated into the finish to add a further aromatic dimension. By contrast, a plastic coating will mask the texture and variation within the wood and, instead of being able to touch a natural material, you will be touching a mixture of synthetic chemicals.

Materials
1/2 cup (100ml) linseed oil
15 drops each of cedarwood, cypress, and pine essential oils

Equipment
Lint-free cloth

Method
Add the scented oils to the linseed oil.

Application
Rub the mixed oils into the wood in the direction of the grain using a lint-free cloth. Repeat several times.

An oiled or waxed finish is naturally antistatic, which means that it is dust and dirt resistant, but oiled or waxed surfaces do need periodic renewal and polishing. If your life's schedule is too hectic to be able to fit in, and enjoy, the process of building up the deep, mellow finish that comes with time, you could use one of the products now on the market that combine natural raw materials with modern technology and low maintenance.

COLORWASHING

Colorwashing bare wood with a thinned emulsion or casein paint will highlight the natural grain in the same way as a wood stain.

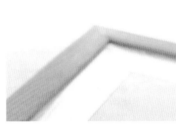

Materials
Thinned colored ecopaint or casein
   paint
Oil and/or furniture wax

Equipment
Paintbrush
Fine sandpaper
Lint-free cloth
Cloth, stiff brush, or very fine steel
   wool

Preparation
Painting wood with a water-based product will raise the grain, making the surface rough, so it is a good idea to raise the grain before you start to apply the colored finish. Do this by brushing warm water onto the surface of the wood, leaving it for a few minutes, and then wiping it off with a cloth. Let the wood dry thoroughly before sanding it lightly to regain a smooth surface.

Application
Brush on the colorwash in the direction of the grain. Before the wash dries, wipe off the surplus with a lint-free cloth to reveal the now colored grain. Let the wash dry thoroughly.

You can protect the surface, making it water-repellent and able to withstand being wiped clean, by finishing it with oil and/or furniture wax. Buff to a soft sheen with a cloth, stiff brush, or some very fine steel wool.

The natural grain of this plain picture frame is
highlighted by the application of a colorwash.

LIMING WITH WAX

Another way of highlighting the natural texture of bare wood is by pushing colored wax into its pores. Traditionally, liming wax was white, but there is no reason why you shouldn't use any other colored pigment to tint the wax.

Materials
Liming wax
Natural pigment

Equipment
Wire brush
Stiff brush
Lint-free cloth

Preparation
Some types of wood are grainier than others and will accept more wax. You can open up the grain with a wire brush, working firmly but carefully in the direction of the grain.

Application
Mix the natural pigment with the wax. Push the wax into the surface of the wood using a stiff brush. Before it dries, remove the surplus by polishing the wood with a lint-free cloth.

Waxing furniture results in an attractive finish that also lets the wood breathe naturally.

DISTRESSED CASEIN

This is a really attractive way to paint wooden furniture, particularly when there are moldings, which this technique emphasizes.

Materials
Colored casein paint
Furniture wax

Equipment
Small paintbrush
Fine steel wool
Soft cloth

Preparation
Paint the piece of furniture with two or three coats of casein paint, letting each coat dry thoroughly before applying the next. You could use different colors for each coat.

Application
Rub lightly with fine steel wool on the entire painted surface to give a smooth finish. Then rub more heavily in certain areas to remove the top layers of paint, thereby revealing lower layers of color or even bare wood in some places. Concentrate on those parts that would naturally receive the hardest wear and tear, such as edges, handles, and moldings.

Wipe off the dust with a soft cloth, and then protect the effect with furniture wax, applied with a cloth and buffed before it is fully dry. The wax will make the color darker.

Distressed casein enhances the natural beauty of
a wooden picture frame.

DISTRESSING WITH A WAX RESIST

A variation on distressed casein (see page 136) is to use smudges of wax, either on the bare wood or between layers of paint, to resist the further application of paint. This makes rubbing off the paint easier.

Rub furniture wax, solid beeswax, or even a candle onto those areas that would normally become chipped or worn most easily. Paint as for distressed casein and, once the paint is fully dry, use a putty knife to take away the layers of paint in the places where you applied the wax. Rub lightly with fine steel wool to remove any remaining bits of wax and to smooth the surface. Protect the surface with oil or furniture wax.

Distressed surfaces look good on traditional
items of furniture, but they could also be used to
add a twist to more modern designs.

MINIMAL DECORATION

CLAY AND PLASTER

If you are undertaking major changes to your home, renovating, or building a new home, and if you will be plastering walls, then serious consideration should be given to self-colored finishes such as clay plaster, polished Venetian plaster, and precolored gypsum plaster. These have the benefit of providing decoration without the need for painting and can result in a variety of attractive textures and finishes.

A further option, worth thinking about if you are using lime plaster on the walls, is to apply colored pigments directly onto the surface of wet plaster—a technique known as fresco.

Although the extraction (mining), processing, and transportation of the ingredients used in all these finishes have an environmental impact, clays and plasters do eliminate the raw material, energy, and financial input involved in the production and application of additional surface coatings.

Clay and plaster work require specialty knowledge and tools, so it is best to employ skilled craftspeople to do this work for you.

Clay plasters are self-colored, eliminating the need for painting after application. They are available in a range of soft colors, such as reds, yellows, and greens.

CLAY PLASTERS

Clay is one of the oldest building materials ever used. This is not surprising, given that it is one of the most common materials on our planet. It is also ecologically friendly: Compared to lime and gypsum, clay production consumes little energy and the end product is easily reincorporated into the environment. Building products made from clay, far from being antiquated, have properties that readily lend themselves to modern buildings and older dwellings alike. Clay has outstanding thermal and vapor-diffusion capacities and, because it "breathes," it contributes to a healthy internal atmosphere. It also absorbs odors and insulates against sound. Warm in winter and cool in summer, clay has a lot going for it.

Unlike other plasters, clay is very forgiving. Whereas gypsum-based plasters must be used quickly once mixed, clay can be left overnight and brought back to life the following day by the addition of a little more water. It also has a longer working time once applied, making it more suitable for experimentation by the amateur.

Clay plasters are typically composed of clay, fine aggregate, organic fibers, and pigment. The inclusion of renewable raw materials like straw and cellulose reduces the amount of clay (which is nonrenewable) needed to cover a given area. In addition, these materials give flexibility to the finish, enabling forms other than flat walls to be built up, and allowing flowing curves to be incorporated into a design.

Clay-based plasters are available in a range of soft colors such as red, yellow, and green. These can be mixed or can have other pigments added to them to produce a more diverse palette. They are suitable for internal surfaces, but should be protected with oils or waxes when used in rooms where they will come into contact with moisture, such as kitchens and bathrooms.

VENETIAN PLASTER— MARMORINO

The skill involved in mixing and applying a Venetian plaster finish has long been passed down through generations of northern Italians. The name marmorino is derived from the Italian word for marble (marmo) and, as this suggests, it is a plaster that includes finely ground marble dust. An extremely durable, low-maintenance finish, true marmorino has a marble content of at least 40 percent. The marble is crushed, ground, washed, and sifted, then mixed with lime putty. It is generally supplied as a ready-mixed paste and, like pure slaked lime, can be stored almost indefinitely in an airtight container.

Marmorino is supplied either in white, which you can tint yourself with lime-tolerant pigments, or as a precolored product. Basic plastering techniques are used in the application, but its particular properties mean that there are differences in the way it is finished. It is essentially burnished using specialty tools, and the extent of the polishing determines the final finish—from matte to highly polished. Walls are thus covered in a layer of stone—limestone and real marble, with its characteristic depth and luster— which makes this product suitable for exterior as well as interior use. Like any stone, the finish "breathes," taking in or giving off humidity according to the surrounding atmosphere.

Marmorino creates a beautiful, durable finish that looks good in any interior.

COLORED NATURAL GYPSUM PLASTERS

These are a relatively new addition to the range of self-colored plasters. They are based on gypsum (hydrated calcium sulfate) and are suitable for application on all building substrates where modern gypsum plasters could be used. Although not as ecologically sound as clay plasters, they are composed of nontoxic (lime-tolerant) pigments and white gypsum and eliminate the necessity of painting.

Suitable for indoor use, natural gypsum plasters are now available in a wide variety of colors and are applied using standard plastering tools and techniques.

Colored natural plasters are now available in a wide variety of colors.

FRESCO

Fresco (the Italian word for "fresh") is a type of mural painting. It is a long and involved technique consisting of three layers of differently textured lime plaster, followed by a final finish. This top layer is composed of lime-tolerant pigments dissolved in lime water, and it is painted onto the final plaster layer while the plaster is still wet. Success depends upon good preparation since every brushstroke is permanent. Lime plaster dries by a process of "carbonation" (see the lime wash recipe on page 62). The pigments get caught up in this process and become integrated with the surface of the plaster, making fresco an extremely durable way of adding color to a wall.

Fresco painting is a perfect example of the processes of building and decorating going hand in hand. Examples of this technique can be found around the world, including Europe, China, India, and Russia. Although examples still survive from the sixteenth century B.C. in Greece and Morocco, the technique had its heyday in Renaissance Italy in the hands of the likes of Leonardo da Vinci, Michelangelo, and Raphael. You may not be living in the Sistine Chapel or be in a position to commission such fine craftsmanship, but even a frescoed border or some blocks of color can be an extremely effective, not to mention low-impact, way of decorating.

It is an exciting prospect indeed that the current resurgence of interest in natural materials and traditional skills may give added impetus to a revival of fresco.

This page: Walls of the bathroom at castle Runkelstein. Top left: A fresco by Fleur Kelly that incorporates elements of ancient Roman frescoes.

This page and opposite: Collections of treasures gathered through the years add a personal touch to a home.

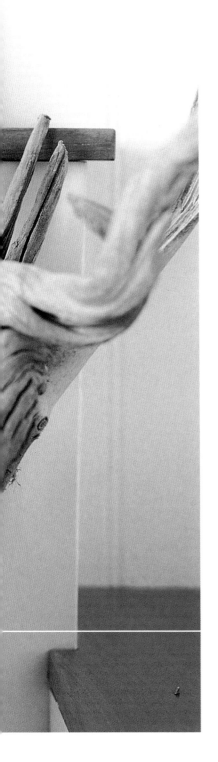

THE HOME AS A PERSONAL SANCTUARY

The house is a perfect expression of the self, and the way we use space is key to understanding our inner selves. The history of human consciousness can be interpreted through our buildings, from the circular shelters of primitive people to contemporary, urban rectangular structures. The square represents man, but is also a symbol of the Earth to which he belongs. The circle represents man's origins. To build a house is to create an area of peace, calm, and security which is a replica of our mother's womb. It is a place where we can leave the world, safe from any external dangers.

Suzy Chiazzari in *The Healing Home*

A starkly minimalist interior is enhanced by the
uneven textured surface of its walls.

Today, the majority of people in the West live in large towns and cities since work in rural areas is now more difficult to find than in the past. Economic and social pressures are continually mounting, especially in urban environments, and so we are more in need than ever of a place of retreat and refuge. How then do we re-create a sense of peace and beauty in our own homes, a sacred space in which to replenish and revive our body, mind, and spirit?

There is an increasing awareness of the need to respect our surroundings in order to be able to provide for a sustainable future. Yet, although many people are aware of the damage that chemical pollutants cause to the environment, far fewer are aware of the extent to which they affect our health and psychological well-being within our own homes. The way in which we relate to our interiors also reflects the quality of our life and our mode of being. William Morris decreed that we should have nothing in our home that we did not know to be useful or believe to be beautiful. We can go further than this by ensuring that the contents of our home, and our home itself, are not only either beautiful or practical but also natural, nonpolluting, and organically healthy.

The humblest of homes can be a source of beauty and health if it is treated with care. Using natural paints on our walls, wood from sustainable plantations, and organic materials made from cotton, linen, or silk all help to bring the natural world back into our home. Certain plants and flowers can even help to keep the air in homes clean and fresh by removing toxic gases from the atmosphere. It has been said that houseplants will be the technology of choice for improving air quality in the twenty-first century. The most valuable plants in this respect are the areca palm (*Chrysalidocarpus lutescens*), the lady palm (*Rhapis excelsa*), the bamboo palm (*Chamaedorea seifrizii*), the rubber plant (*Ficus elastica*), and Dracaena "Janet Craig" (*Dracaena deremensis*).

In order to create a healing space, we should provide nourishment for all our senses. The scent of essential oils can not only make a room smell beautiful, it also acts as a therapeutic agent, purifying the air and keeping infections at bay. Music soothes the soul, and a fountain or water

feature makes a gentle sound while at the same time creating negative ions, which help to dispel any stress or tension. Healthy food is essential, while our awareness of different textures and shapes feeds our sense of touch. Treasures brought back from weekends away in the country or on our travels can also help to bring the richness of our experience directly into our own home. Exotic furnishings, paintings, and individual ornaments or pieces of furniture can be found in local markets nowadays and often mirror the life of the spirit more surely than any mass-produced object. Finally, by choosing natural paints to put on our walls, with their subtle texture and appearance and often pleasant smell, we will be nourishing our senses on a variety of levels simultaneously.

Our home is therefore a retreat from the outside world, an extension of the natural world, and a sanctuary that reflects our own growth and development. In this way, it takes on a living, ever-changing quality and, as such, it can provide a source of fertile inspiration and respite to those who live there, as well as all who visit.

THE ART OF FENG SHUI

Feng shui is the Taoist art and science of living in harmony with our environment. It is the ancient skill of achieving perfect equilibrium with nature and has been used for over 4,000 years. In the East, people have relied on it to design cities, build homes and businesses, and organize their interiors. Over the centuries it has developed hundreds of different formulas to solve all kinds of problems relating to the interconnection between ourselves and our surroundings. With feng shui we can change, harmonize, or energize our lives. Applied correctly, it can help us to choose an appropriate career, increase our prosperity, find satisfying relationships, resolve difficulties, and create a beautiful place in which to live.

The core of feng shui is the theory of the five elements, whose basic principles are simple and easy to apply. Fire (heat), water, wood, earth, and metal are almost everywhere we look. They interact constantly, either supporting or destroying each other, and in an individual sense, our health depends upon establishing the

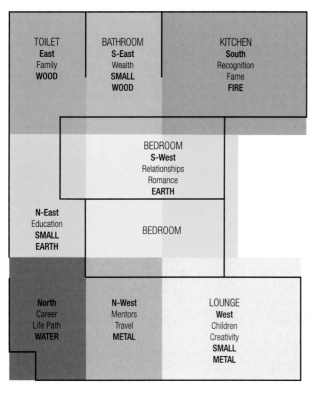

TOILET **East** Family **WOOD**	**BATHROOM** **S-East** Wealth **SMALL** **WOOD**	**KITCHEN** **South** Recognition Fame **FIRE**

EARTH
Yellow, orange,
terra-cotta, naturals

METAL
White, silver, gold

WATER
Blue, black

WOOD
Green, brown

FIRE
Red, pink

BEDROOM
S-West
Relationships
Romance
EARTH

N-East
Education
SMALL
EARTH

BEDROOM

North
Career
Life Path
WATER

N-West
Mentors
Travel
METAL

LOUNGE
West
Children
Creativity
SMALL
METAL

1.

2.

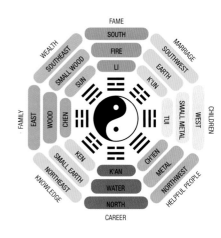

Relations between the elements.

1.
Creative circle: fire creates earth (ash), earth creates metal (minerals), metal creates water, water creates wood, wood creates fire.
2.
Destructive/controlling: fire melts metal, metal chops wood, wood penetrates earth, earth limits water.

correct balance between them. Each element is represented by a different spectrum of light, so by using the appropriate color in the right place in our interiors, we can help to create balance and abundance in our lives.

There are two major schools of feng shui:

– *The Form School, where the emphasis is on the shapes of landforms such as hills and mountains, the positions of trees and bushes, and the orientations and directions of waterways.*

– *The Compass School, based on the eight Trigrams of the* I Ching *and the nine-grid* lo shu *magic square, which emphasizes the importance of the compass directions and locations.*

Both schools are important and valuable, but if we are looking for simple solutions to our everyday problems, the theory of the five elements, with their corresponding colors, which belongs to the Compass School and its Eight Mansions formula, is perfect.

Within this formula, each Trigram has its own meaning and place, and each represents a different family member, compass direction, and element. They are arranged around the sides of the octagonal *pa kua* or can be placed within the *lo shu* magic square with their corresponding numbers (see diagram). The meanings of the Trigrams relate very closely to our lives with their various aspects.

On the drawing you can see how each Trigram relates to a compass direction, an element, a color, and a specific aspect of our lives. In order to apply the *lo shu* square to the plan of your house, simply stand in the middle of your house and take a reading from a compass. Be aware of any metal objects in the room, as they will deflect the compass needle. Once you have aligned the magic square with the plan of your house, you will be able to see which element dominates each room. For example, if your living room is in the southwest part of the house, the best colors to use in this space are the earthy pigments, such as deep yellows, oranges, and terra-cottas. Burnt umber, burnt sienna, and yellow ocher are all naturally derived earth pigments that evoke richness and warmth and are very effective used in layered washes. Red is also indicated because red is the color of fire, which supports earth (see diagram). The southwest represents marriage, romantic happiness, and relationships in general. This is a good position for a bedroom. The main color to avoid in this room is green, since wood destroys earth (see diagram).

A certain room may contain two sections, such as south/southeast, fire/wood, red/green. Which color do we use in this room and how do we create a correct balance? We can use both colors in this case, but the dominant color should be green, since wood (green) is the mother of fire. If we use too much red, the fire will exhaust the wood, which means that we would tend to spend more than we earn. A positive relationship with wealth depends upon the right balance between these two elements (see diagram).

Color remedies are only a small part of feng shui. Sometimes it is better to use neutral colors and to energize the room by using such things as plants (wood), water features, candles (fire), and wind chimes (metal). If, for example, your bedroom is in the eastern part of the house, with little light but a beautiful garden outside, there is no point in using green (wood) on the walls, since this might create a rather cold and unpleasant feeling. The wood element is already present in the green of the garden, so in this case it would be better to use neutral colors or sunshine yellow (earth, which helps wood to grow) with some green accents. For example, room features could be picked out in verdigris, the beautiful bluish green natural pigment extensively used by artists in Greece and Rome and found on the walls of Pompeii. On the other hand, a beautiful green in a southeast-facing study can help to energize our thoughts and "grow" new ideas.

Feng shui might seem rigid and guided by many rules, but as we go deeper into the subject we can discover a sense of freedom and space. We become aware that things "coincidentally" fit into the right place. The key point is to understand the precise quality of each of the five elements: how they react with each other and how to balance them. Too much or too little of anything is never advisable. We can turn bad fortune into good, create harmony and abundance in our lives if we use the right principles along with common sense.

Maciek Sikora
Feng shui consultant

Soft pink walls are complemented by sheer blinds, creating a restful and tranquil atmosphere.

THE PRINCIPLES OF DECORATION

There are a number of principles that facilitate the good design and decor of any house. If they are taken into account at the outset of the planning stage, it will be far easier to obtain a harmonious and pleasing result.

THE USE OF SPACE

The first principle to keep in mind when considering any kind of design idea is space. Start by assessing the fundamental structure of the property and the way in which the space is divided. The Victorians felt very strongly that we needed different rooms for different functions, but we have freed ourselves from this notion dramatically in recent years. Some rooms, for example, may benefit from being combined with others to form one larger room. By knocking down the wall between a separate sitting room and a kitchen, for example, it is possible to make one large open-plan living area. Multipurpose and open-plan living is not a new idea: it has its roots in the hall house of earlier centuries and has now regained its popularity, providing a more fluid and sociable way of living and working.

Apart from assessing the overall structure, it is also vital to think about how the structure will be used and the function that each room will fulfil. Will it be used as a quiet space for retreating and relaxing? Is it to be a stimulating area used by the whole family and for entertaining? Is it to be set aside solely for use as a study or work area? Do certain rooms need to be multipurpose and therefore multidimension, i.e., a study during the week and a guest room on the weekends? All these questions need to be answered before you move on to consider other factors such as style, lighting, and color.

STYLE AND FEATURES

Defining the style or period of decoration is the next major decision. Do you prefer a warm and light Mediterranean-style home, a classical interior, one with an Oriental bias, a rural country-house atmosphere, or the sleek minimalist lines of a modern design? The choices seem endless. Synchronizing one style throughout the house usually makes decorating easier and gives a harmonious sense of design, and the architecture of one's home is generally the guide for choosing this particular style. With ingenuity, however, you can combine styles within one house. If you live on two floors or more, each floor could be designed differently. For example, a classically designed living room and kitchen on one floor could be combined with modern bedrooms on another floor, providing a stimulating contrast. If a mixture of styles is used, even in the case of adjoining rooms, these can still be harmonized through the use of color, either by using harmonizing tones or by contrasting them with those at the other end of the color spectrum (see the color wheel on page 164).

Once the style of decoration has been chosen, you should then look closely at the outstanding features of each room. If, for example, there is a beautiful marble fireplace, it can act as the central focus for a room. Does the room have a large bay window or classical cornices and moldings? Traditional features are always highly valued and can always be restored if they have been taken out. If the room has a beautiful view, this should be made into a feature. Conversely, you also need to look at the drawbacks. If the room suffers from too little light and has small windows, these can be remedied through the judicious use of color. How high are the ceilings? If they are too high, either chair rails or picture rails can be used to give a sense of reducing the height. Equally, if they are low and the room feels cramped, use color and lighting to create a sense of space and height.

Another way to approach decoration is to look at different parts of a room as an individual vignette. See each section as a painting or a photograph that stands on its own. What can be added to make it more interesting or more dramatic? What is lacking? Equally, what can be taken away in order to keep a sense of simplicity and peace? Nothing should be superfluous in any design. Less is frequently more in term of design aesthetic. Be sure that materials and color used in each section of the house link up in some way with other parts of the house.

LIGHT AND LIGHTING

Natural light is the next consideration—and a crucial one. The early Greeks considered it so important that they made access to sunlight a legal right. With this in mind, check every room for the direction it faces. For example, a room facing west or south will have far more warm light than a north- or east-facing room. We are now more aware of the impact light has on our mood. Seasonal Affective Disorder,

An ancient wooden niche in a converted barn is
set off by the use of flame-colored lime paint.

Left and above: Be bold with color! Mix and match toning and contrasting colors for greater effect.

known as S.A.D., affects some people when they are subjected to low levels of light, particularly in the wintry days of the northern hemisphere. We should, therefore, try to make the maximum use of light and sunlight in all our rooms. This can be done in a number of ways, such as by using reflected light and mirrors, but it can also be done through the careful use of color.

Yellow has the highest reflectivity of any color. Cadmium yellow, originally made from the naturally occurring silvery metal cadmium, was used extensively by landscape painters, including Claude Monet, for its opaque brilliance and purity of color. Later, Hansa yellows were made in Germany in the early twentieth century from organic pigments. More intense than cadmium yellow, they are semitransparent and have great value for glazing.

Another key element is that of lighting. Overhead lighting is definitely the least attractive, although the most frequently used. More appealing are either table lamps, creating pools of light, or spotlights, which can be used for reading by or to accentuate a feature in the room. Uplights, which softly illuminate an area of the wall, or directional downlights, are also very effective. A chandelier or a pretty wrought iron light can make a decorative centerpiece, and there are also ornate and decorative wall lights echoing different styles, such as Art Nouveau or the Elizabethan period. The choice of lighting is enormous and fascinating to explore, as well as being crucial to creating the type of atmosphere desired.

The type of bulbs used is also very important because they can affect the quality of light. Tungsten bulbs, for example, emit a warm

light, while so-called daylight bulbs, which bring back the equivalent of natural daylight into a room, are colder and brighter. Dimmers are indispensable to set a mood but they cannot be used with daylight bulbs. With the judicious use of lighting, it is possible to highlight the good features of a room and disguise those that are not so pleasing. At night, of course, the most enchanting lighting is always produced by candlelight, which can transform any room into a romantic haven.

COLOR

Having taken all these factors into account, the exciting imaginative work now begins with choosing colors. Color, above all, can set the period of a room and create a mood. Used skillfully, it can create pattern and texture where needed. It also sets the tone for whether a

Above and below: Color shouldn't be limited to paints and soft furnishings. Floors and doors can all have their share, too.

room is to be stimulating or restful, according to your needs. In short, color is the most immediate and transformative element in a room; yet, unlike structure, it can easily be changed if you tire of a certain scheme.

With the clever use of color, a small, dark room can appear larger and lighter, while a very large room can become cozy and warm. Color can also be used to change the shape of a room or to make it more lively—such as by painting it in elegant stripes. Color can optically lift the height of a ceiling if light-reflecting colors such as yellow are used. By contrast, a deep red, blue, or

purple ceiling will help to bring down the height of the ceiling. Working with natural paints and pigments is different than working with synthetically derived products. They have a more subtle, inner luminosity, along with more variety in finished texture and effect.

Continuity in the color scheme can link the overall design of the house together when harmonizing colors can be seen from one room to the next. Even if adjoining rooms are not painted the same color, a harmony of tone will emphasize a continuity of design. "Color," of course, includes both white and the softer off-whites, which can be stunning if combined in a room, with different shades of white predominating both on the walls and in the furnishings to create the epitome of restful elegance.

Color can also suggest a particular period: the neoclassical eighteenth-century period used pastel and muted pinks or murky greens; the Victorians liked dark rich colors, while whitewashed plaster and terra-cotta evoke the timeless Mediterranean look. Brilliant colors, such as lapis lazuli or emerald green, point to an Islamic or North African influence, while the English country house uses faded colors, such as old rose, to perfection.

Historical trends were largely based on the availability of materials, since at one time all paint was made from entirely natural substances. Different countries and regions thus tended to rely on those pigments that were found locally. The rich, soft Mediterranean colors, for example, include the famous terra di Siena from Tuscany and burnt umber from Umbria, both in Italy. Sienna and umber are key colors

Left: Dusty-pink walls perfectly complement this playful corner.

for creating effects of depth quite impossible to achieve with modern chemical paints. With imagination and some research into specific historical periods, we can easily pinpoint the appropriate colors used to evoke a certain period in history. Alternatively, we can look to contemporary ideas for interior decoration, since what is happening in the world of fashion is always a useful indication of color trends.

Besides using paint to change the mood of a room dramatically, we can also change throws and furnishings seasonally to emphasize either the lightness of summer or the need for warmth in winter. Both color and texture play their part in providing such contrasts: crimson throws, combined with deep chocolate brown or amber cushions, can give instant warmth in the colder months, while in summer, linen and unbleached calico curtains, together with airy sky-blue and light green furnishings, will help to evoke long, hazy, sun-filled days.

MATERIALS

Once the use of space, light, style, and color have been determined, the other crucial factor in decoration is the use of materials. For example, a Shaker-like style of decoration would rely on bare wooden floorboards, subtly colored or neutral plain walls, and highly crafted but simple furniture. By contrast, a Rococo-style decor would use gold and elaborate decoration in the form of trellises and arches to suggest a sense of lighthearted and playful delight. Trompe l'oeil can add sophistication and a sense of illusion to pretty, dusty pink or pastel walls. In this type of interior, furniture and furnishings would need to be elaborate and flirtatious to match. Diverse combinations of style can also be juxtaposed in imaginative ways to create a delightfully uncontrived and homey effect, as opposed to the formality of style in more co-ordinated designs. Above all, have fun experimenting and remember that everything can be changed, especially a coat of paint.

Sahasrara:
the crown chakra

Ajna:
the third-eye chakra

Vishuddha:
the throat chakra

Anahata:
the heart chakra

Manipura:
the solar plexus chakra

Swadhishthana:
the naval/sacral chakra

Muladhara:
the root/base chakra

COLOR THERAPY FOR INTERIORS

In the past 30 years there has been a revival of interest in color. It is already becoming widely accepted that color has a profound effect on our health and general sense of well-being. We all know which colors we like and which we dislike, but despite colors pervading almost every area of our lives, what do we actually know about how they affect us?

In ancient civilizations, color was highly significant and was used symbolically for religious, artistic, and healing purposes. During the Middle Ages, for example, an orange mineral called minium (or red lead) was used to provide the rich opaque pigments frequently used in illuminated manuscripts. Orange, like gold, was associated with the sun, with opulence or wealth, and with inner wisdom. Today, constantly changing fashions largely dictate which colors we should wear or how to paint our homes, while advertising has discovered how to use color to sell products. On the other hand, a growing awareness that color has the power to influence the inner condition of a person, or transform the atmosphere of a place, is leading to a new approach to interior design and decorating.

Besides a subjective response to the individual colors, there are objective qualities inherent in each of them. We can all feel the calming effect of blue, the lightness of yellow, and the intensity and heat of red. We also know that we "get the blues," "go green with envy," and "see red." In this way, we sense the duality within every color, and therefore their ability to have a positive or negative effect on us. This is the principle on which color therapy for interiors is based.

From a scientific point of view, color is a manifestation of light. Sunlight is composed of a range of color vibrations, each with a different speed and wavelength. Each color is energy vibrating on a different wavelength. Wherever light meets darkness or matter, color arises. We can see this clearly when the sun shines through the rain onto a backdrop of dark gray clouds and a rainbow appears, or in the evenings, when the balance of light and dark makes the colors appear most intense.

A rainbow has red light at the top and violet at the bottom, with all the other colors in between. This is because red has the slowest and longest wavelength, and violet vibrates fastest and has the shortest wavelength. We absorb these color vibrations into our systems through our eyes, our skin, and our auras. The aura acts like a prism for light, breaking it up into seven different colors, which in turn nourish our seven main chakras, or energy centers, which are located along the spine from the base to the crown of our heads (see diagram).

Each chakra, which is a bit like a radio station receiving an energy frequency, is related to different body organs, functions, and emotions. From the bottom going up toward the heart we have red, orange, and yellow, the warm end of the spectrum and the daytime range, stimulating activity and connecting us to the world around us. From the crown of our heads toward our hearts we have violet, indigo, and blue, the cooler colors and night range, which relate more to our inner lives and rest. Holding the balance between the cool blues and the warm yellows is green, located in our heart chakra. With this system in mind, we can more easily choose colors that will assist the activity or function of a room. A general guideline is to have the warmer and more active, stimulating colors downstairs and the cooler, more restful colors upstairs.

Experiments in America with blind people proved that spending time in an all-red room and an all-blue room affected body temperature, blood pressure, pulse rate, and moods differently. Another experiment in Canada involved people walking into rooms that were identical except for their color. Their emotional responses were recorded and huge differences of experience were noted purely as a result of the color.

In the same way that we need a balance of different foods in order to maintain good health, we also need to be exposed to a balance of color energies to nourish different aspects of our being. Regardless of whether we like a color or not, each color wavelength has an important and specific contribution to make to our physical, emotional, mental, and spiritual health. However, just like anything that has the potential to be of benefit to us, the wrong usage or combination of colors can actually harm us when taken to extremes.

Red, for example, is the most stimulating of colors. The small quantities of red found in berries, rosy cheeks, and a red rose all suggest health, warmth, love, and nurturing. Red becomes extremely dramatic in larger quantities, however, such as a field of poppies or a sunset. Red also has the inherent ability to evoke in us a sense of prohibition, rebellion, or possible danger. The mural artists of Pompeii used rare and expensive cinnabar brought from mines in Almaden, Spain, to create bright, rich, high-impact reds on their walls. A form of mercury, cinnabar was also hazardous to the health.

Our immediate association with green may be that it is the color of life and has a calming or balancing effect—like being in a green field or forest. We may think of fresh, healthy lettuce, spring leaves, and grass. When we paint a room green, however, it may prove to be claustrophobic and deadening. Green, when it is not imbued with life, assumes its shadow side, as found in the green of a stagnant pond or the complexion of a sick person. Despite being the color most closely associated with natural life, green is a difficult color to use in the home. To reproduce the qualities found in nature with

This page: Green has a calming effect and, when used in dining rooms, may encourage restfulness and therefore digestion.
Opposite: An unpretentious and beautiful pale blue stairway.

paint is extremely difficult, as many artists will confirm. This is partly because in nature there are thousands of shades of green blending together, shining through each other and offsetting other colors. Few green pigments are found naturally, exceptions being terre-verte, verdigris, and emerald green—a poisonous copper aceto-arsenite also used as a rat poison in the sewers of Paris.

Green is a color that has a tendency to become dense and heavy and make one feel sluggish unless it is able to "move." A wall painted with a flat green can appear rigid and stagnant. If, however, the green is applied in layers of transparent natural colorwashes, it gives the impression of being filled with movement and light and has a healthy look about it. This principle is also true of other colors. Movement within the colors, as achieved through washes, textures, and certain old techniques, always gives the light the opportunity to play with the color and create subtle but beautiful effects. Alternatively, a stronger flat green can be fine if it does not rise much above waist level or if paintings, moldings, or other wall fixtures break it up. It works well in rooms where activity is not to be encouraged.

Flat greens can be counter-balanced by the use of bright red to enliven them. It was, incidentally, this combination that the Impressionists used in their paintings to make nature come alive. Previously, green trees and grass had been painted in subdued greens or browns, and so the essence of nature—life and living things—was omitted. The Impressionists began to introduce tiny splashes of red, the complementary color to green,

thereby creating the sensation of movement. By using red, the color of life, they managed to enliven the green so that it never appeared stagnant. This is what we need to be aware of when using green in our homes.

As soon as a green tends toward blue, it moves away from the fresh feel of living, growing things. Blue, in terms of the chakra system, is connected to the "third eye," which is situated between our eyes. It is the chakra related to our intellectual abilities and our intuitive insights. When it is not too strong or dark, it is a restful color that encourages us to let go and expand our consciousness. It allows us to drift into states of relaxation through its quiet nature. Blues encourage deeper and more serious conversations rather than light and cheerful ones. Think of the vast blue of a clear sky or a huge expanse of blue ocean stretching toward the horizon. On the other hand, peacock blues have an exoticism about them that demand attention and admiration, again drawing us away from ourselves. The blues encourage us to become slightly detached from our bodies. Until the beginning of the eighteenth century, the only blue pigments were made from semiprecious stones such as lapis lazuli and azurite, or a ground cobalt blue known as smalt. Blue was once considered a status symbol, and the color blue still implies a certain nobility of thought.

Colors can be divided into three main groups: those that stimulate and uplift, those that relax and calm, and those that provide harmony or balance. Every color also has a warm or a cool shade: dove gray, for example, has a warm effect, while steel gray is cooling (see page 164). When

painted on the walls of a room, colors can create warmth or coolness; they can also make a room look bigger or smaller, darker or lighter.

So, having taken a number of things into consideration when decorating a room, such as the size of the space, the amount of light, the function of the room, and the style and mood we wish to create, we finally, and most importantly, need to consider the needs of the people who use it. We are all different, so it is difficult to meet the physical and emotional needs of everybody using the room. We can,

Above: Several different colors are used here, but the overall effect is restful because the colors do not compete for attention with each other.

however, choose colors that support the activities taking place within it. A home office, for example, will need colors that support communication, clarity of thought, objectivity, and cooperation, while the colors for a kitchen should stimulate social interaction, assist the digestive processes, inspire creativity, and provide a warm and friendly welcome to each new day. A consultation with a professional color consultant can help to determine individual needs and select appropriate colors.

DESIGNING WITH COLOR

Apart from objective effects, the use of color is also something very personal. It stimulates our senses, influences our mood, and helps create a particular atmosphere. How we respond to an individual color depends on our temperament—extroverts tend to feel happy with bold colors, while introverts prefer more subdued colors. Through using specific combinations of color, combined with a careful consideration of

light, furnishing materials, and structural proportions, we can create a home that is welcoming, supportive, and comfortable.

The colors with which we surround ourselves will without doubt have an effect on us, and so it is important to feel comfortable with our choice. However, I can definitely recommend trying out new colors and letting them grow on you. It can be amazing how a new area of life opens up as a result of exposing yourself to a new color energy. I never liked pink until I found myself house-sitting and unwittingly spending time in a bedroom with vibrant pink curtains. Each morning I woke up bathed in pink light. The sense of relaxation, nurturing, and warmth had such a profound effect on me that I painted my own bedroom an old rose

color and have loved the atmosphere of the room ever since. And if you really don't like a color, well, you can always paint over it.

Angela Findlay
Color therapist

Simple color schemes are often the most effective. Try not to use more than one or two principal colors in a room, as well as a contrasting or complementary tone. The best way to choose a background color for the room is to experiment with a palette of different shades and nuances, in combination with the colors and textures of the furniture and materials. Remember that the overall color scheme of a home has to be in harmony.

The walls define the space in a room, while the colors, to a large degree, define the mood. Colored

Above and left: Two glorious displays of color and inventiveness, one on plaster and the other on wood.

walls are similar to background music: each color tone is like a musical note and, as in music, some tones can create a harmonious chord while others grate with each other. It is not only a question of which colors to put together, however, because the quality of a color is also important. Choose too strong a tone, and the walls may dominate the room like loud music or they may compete for attention with the other colors used. Choose too soft a tone, however, and the overall effect could become sickly. Color is energy, so a disharmonious chord of color tones will cause us to "wince" on an energetic level, and our inner sense of harmony will be affected. Extended exposure to a limited or unhealthy palette of colors can lead to an energetic imbalance. Many emotional and mental disturbances are greatly exacerbated by exposure to the "wrong" colors or combinations.

Colors also need light and a sense of movement, often provided by texture. Some colors become fully alive only when combined with a particular material or when exposed to a certain level of light. Visually, we experience how the light plays with the texture. A glossy or glazed surface, for example, looks much brighter than a matte finish, and these effects are particularly apparent when working with organic products. Light changes the character of space and is one of the most important factors to work with in any design, in addition to the balance between hard and soft textures.

The relatively modern method of using a roller to achieve a perfectly uniform surface of color often leads to colors appearing dense and rigid. Nowhere in nature do we find large expanses of a single color. If we apply colors in a more living way, allowing them to "breathe," our walls literally become enlivened, and as living

beings ourselves, we respond better to them. There are many ways of making colors breathe and therefore appear more alive. Using natural ingredients gives the colors a wonderful vibrancy that chemical ones cannot match. Natural pigments can be mixed with a transparent glaze for colorwashing or can be added to a number of other natural materials, such as lime washes,

casein paint, tempera, and ready-made ecopaints, to give beautiful, rich finishes.

Paint colors are generally chosen by reference to color charts or swatches in a store. Sometimes, when the paint is used at home, the colors look different and do not create the effect that was originally imagined. This is partly because colors are affected by the light and

shade from natural and artificial lighting, and also by the colors of furnishings in the room in which they are used. A useful function of natural pigments is that they can be used to alter the color of store-bought paints if they are not quite what was wanted. Another way of using them is to buy a base of white ecopaint and to color this yourself with natural pigments.

If you are inexperienced or lacking in confidence about mixing your own colors, there is a tool that can help. The color wheel is a really useful device that shows not only how colors are made by combination, but also how different colors relate to and affect each other. It is simple to use once some basic principles are understood. All the colors are made from various combinations of red, yellow, and blue. These are known as the primary colors because they cannot be mixed from any other colors. When two primaries are mixed together in various proportions, they form the secondary colors of orange, green, and violet. Likewise, when a primary color is mixed with a secondary color, the result is a tertiary color.

PRIMARIES

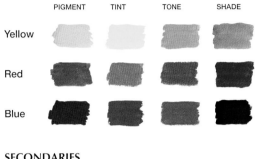

	PIGMENT	TINT	TONE	SHADE
Yellow				
Red				
Blue				

SECONDARIES

	PIGMENT	TINT	TONE	SHADE
Orange				
Violet				
Green				

ADD WATER | ADD WHITE PAINT | ADD GRAY (OR WHITE AND BURNT UMBER) | ADD BLACK (FROM BURNT UMBER)

TERTIARIES

Red + orange = red–orange
Yellow + green = yellow–green
Blue + violet = blue–violet

Yellow + orange = yellow–orange
Blue + green = blue–green
Red + violet = red–violet

WARM AND COOL COLORS

Reds, oranges, and yellows are the warm, or advancing, colors. Greens, blues, and violets are the cool, or receding, colors.

TINTS, TONES, AND SHADES

Adding white to a color results in a tint. If you are adding natural pigment to a ready-made white paint, you will always be working with tints of the original pigment color. Adding gray to a color results in a tone, and adding black results in a shade of the original.

COMPLEMENTARIES

The colors that lie directly opposite each other on the color wheel are known as complementaries.

Blue – orange
Yellow – violet
Red–violet – yellow–green

Red – green
Blue–violet – yellow–orange
Red–orange – blue–green

NEUTRALS

Like black and white, when two complementary colors are mixed together, the result will be a gray, or neutral.

HARMONY AND CONTRAST

Colors that appear closest together on the color wheel harmonize, e.g., blue is harmonious with blue–violet or blue–green. The farther apart they appear on the wheel, the more they will contrast, e.g., blue contrasts most with orange (its complementary color). Complementaries are useful because they enhance each other—a blue stenciled detail, for example, would bring out the orangeness of an orange wall.

Tints, tones, and shades of neutrals will harmonize with either of the complementaries from which they are made. This can be useful when choosing colors to harmonize with furnishings, for example.

Armed with this basic color theory, you are now equipped to choose and mix your own color schemes. Remember that the color wheel is an idealized situation based on pure colors. When examined closely, it can be seen that natural pigments are not pure but are composed of a number of different colors. Ultramarine blue, for example, contains some red.

It is advisable to experiment with small amounts of pigment and paint first, in order to get a feel for the materials. Keep your combinations simple to begin with, to avoid ending up with muddy colors. Also, you will quickly discover that different pigments vary in terms of their coloring strength. Some, such as oxide red, are very powerful, and only a very small amount may be needed. Keep a record of your experiments so that you can reproduce successful results on a larger scale.

A field of ripening barley rippling in the breeze inspired the pale gold color of my hall, and the bleached peachy cream colors in my bathroom were the colors of a favorite shell. The associations the colors evoke fill me with the mood I wish to create, and with that in mind, I set to work on the walls applying the paint or glaze with sponges and brushes. Once the walls are covered, I look for ways of enhancing certain features with details painted in freehand. A color on its own usually creates a sense of one-sidedness and calls for its complimentary color in order to really "sing." Additional colors in the form of cushions, paintings, curtains, etc., can greatly enhance the overall effect.

Angela Findlay *color therapist*

The modern kitchen is a multi-functional room
that must be adapted to the needs of its users.

DESIGN SUGGESTIONS FOR EVERY ROOM

The Kitchen

As discussed in the previous chapter, choices of color, style, and decor of a room all depend largely on the amount of light available, the size and function of the room, the desired atmosphere, and the needs or preferences of those who use it. In the case of a kitchen, there are several different aspects to take into consideration because the modern kitchen is a multifunctional room as well as a place of regular and diverse activity. Let us look at the main requirements or functions, and then discuss the colors and designs that would most support them.

Above and right: Rich earth tones, from yellows through pinks to terra-cottas, are creative colors which bring instant warmth into the kitchen.

In former times, the heart of the home was located around the hearth. It was the warm center around which people would gather to cook, socialize, and eat. Today, the whole kitchen, instead of just the cooking area, has become the heart of the home: the room in which our basic survival needs are met and in which families come together for a variety of activities. In recent times, it has become increasingly common for men to share the task of cooking, thus making the kitchen no longer the almost exclusive domain of women.

Changes have also taken place in trends for entertaining, with many evening meals being less formal affairs—more likely a casual supper than a dinner party. Today, many people like to have one room that serves as both kitchen and dining area, or opt for an open-plan arrangement whereby the cook can join in the premeal socializing as well. So the kitchen is not only used for preparing and cooking food but is also a place for gathering, sharing, and relaxing together with friends or family.

When designing a kitchen, the most important consideration to take into account is that it is primarily a workshop, having a practical function. The inclusion and arrangement of enough work surfaces is therefore of paramount importance, since most people use their kitchen for the preparation of two or three meals a day. Easy access to utensils, ingredients, and all the things needed on a daily basis is essential.

Good lighting is also vital in the working areas. It is always best to avoid fluorescent lighting, however, not only in the kitchen but elsewhere in the home, because it gives off an ultraviolet, bluish light that cools any other colors in the room. Such a cooling effect is at odds with the warm and nurturing role of the kitchen as the heart of the home, as well as being potentially unhealthy. (Fluorescent bulbs send out subtle, pulsing vibrations that can disturb our nervous system and, through their quickening effect, make us hyperactive or irritable.) In the kitchen, it is best to use full-spectrum lighting, a form of artificial light that imitates daylight.

It takes inspiration, enthusiasm, and creativity to prepare food that is tasty and nourishing, and the best colors to support this creative process are the rich earth tones from orange through to golden yellow, as well as all the beautiful terra-cotta and peach colors. The yellow and orange tones help to bring instant warmth and light into a room and are especially valuable where natural light is lacking. Orange is also a very joyful color that encourages us to be bold, try out new things, and enjoy what we are doing. These warm colors are also thought to aid the digestive processes.

Other colors appropriate for kitchens are warm creams, ochers, pale wheat colors, and certain reds. Cream tones have a soft warmth about them that makes them very comfortable to live with at all times. Creams and pale yellows also respond well to candlelight and don't jump out, demanding attention. In a kitchen, where there are plenty of things

demanding immediate attention, from boiling saucepans to hungry children, it is advisable to use colors that help to induce a sense of calm and ease. Reds have to be used with care in this context, since very strong tones can be uncomfortable to live with—let alone wake up to first thing in the morning.

Suitable paints for the kitchen include hard-wearing, washable, even scrubbable ecopaints. If you want to use casein paint, then it needs to be protected with a glaze so that you can wipe it clean. Bear in mind, however, that if casein is used in a frequently damp area, such as above the sink or stovetop, it will revert to its basic sour milk origins and begin to smell. Lime paints may seem like an odd choice in a kitchen because they are not washable and will mark easily with any splash of grease, but they do have mild antiseptic qualities.

THE DINING AREA

If you have a dining area in a kitchen, or an open-plan arrangement, it is preferable to have the dining area slightly apart from the main activity area. This provides a sense of peace and relaxation away from the work that goes into preparing and

clearing up the food. A separate dining room will provide this naturally.

Eating is not only an essential part of our daily lives, it is also a potentially pleasurable social event. Mealtimes are occasions when a huge amount of our energy is invested in the functions of the body, and research has shown that laughter and the enjoyment of food assist the digestive processes. Our metabolic rate affects the speed at which we can process what we eat and the extent to which we can transform food into energy, as opposed to fat.

Scientific tests have shown that the color red significantly speeds up our pulse rate and increases the efficiency of our metabolism. Red is also the color that links us to our roots and our blood families, while orange is a color that is connected to our relationships and how we communicate with others. Reds and oranges help to put us in touch with our bodies and generate warmth in a room: They are in harmony and reflect the colors of the element fire and of the hearth. Both these colors are therefore supportive to dining areas and kitchens, especially rich reds with plum or coral tints and golden orange tones.

Left: Warm colors such as orange are thought to aid the digestive process and so are ideal for dining areas.

The dining room is often the showplace for very personal ideas of luxury and comfort, such as this theatrical design.

The kitchen and dining areas are social and public spaces, however, and it is advisable to take the comfort of friends and guests into consideration. Red is a color that many people find over-powering—or even threatening—for a variety of reasons. So, if you are intent on using red in the dining area or dining room, try to tone it down to a rich, mellow hue, or let it sink into the luxurious velvety tones of burgundy, which have looked wonderful in dining areas for decades.

Color choices also depend on temperament and lifestyle. Breakfast is a meal that is sometimes rushed while at other times may be enjoyed at a more leisurely pace. A refreshing color can help to start the day with a lift. This would be ideal for a person who has trouble waking up or whose job requires an early start. The brighter shades of orange, peach, or apricot have an immediately uplifting effect, as do all the warm yellows. Yellow also has a certain youth about it, which is appropriate for the younger part of the day, but can have a jarring effect on the senses if it becomes too lemony, bright, or acidic. Yellow stimulates mental activity, but in excess it can also promote nervousness or agitation. Care is therefore needed in selecting exactly the right type of yellow to suit each individual situation.

A dining area that is used primarily in the evening requires a different ambience. Rich, luminous colors, set off by candles or low lighting, will help to give the room a dramatic yet intimate atmosphere. Certain tones of green, the complementary color to red, can help to provide a fresh feel, especially in the form of plants or decorative details. Warm tones are also ideal for families with children and those for whom the dining table doubles as a place of creative activity throughout the day. The associations of restfulness that accompany blue, the complementary color to orange, make it a good choice for curtains or evening tableware.

The type of paint you choose for the dining room really depends on a number of factors, such as whether or not your children (or your friends) are liable to be splashing food about, in which case you need a washable surface. Completely flat finishes, such as casein, size-base paint, or matte ecopaint, will not be as durable as a wall paint that dries to a soft sheen. The ceiling, at least, could be painted with a matte finish. You could consider painting the area matte throughout, then protecting the most vulnerable areas with a glaze. This would work well with casein because the effect of the glaze darkening the color could be incorporated into your design.

THE LIVING ROOM

The main purpose of the living room is relaxation. It is a place to be alone or with others at the end of the day or at weekends. It is a space in which to unwind, let go of work-related issues, and indulge in other interests, hobbies, or conversation. Some of the more common features found in living rooms are a television, a stereo, a fireplace, sofas and armchairs, and possibly bookshelves. All these inspire passivity on a physical level, and rest. The living room is the area of the house that stylistically most often reflects our personality and interests. It is also a place where we like to feel comfortable, protected, warm, and safe.

The design of your living room will be dictated partly by the age and style of your house or apartment, and partly by very personal ideas of what makes a space comfortable. High or low ceilings, small or large windows, carpets or bare floorboards are usually dictated by the type of home in which you live, but the interior design and color scheme are up to you.

It may be that you live in an old building but prefer modern furniture, in which case a clever and considered use of contemporary materials, such as glass or metal, could lead to highly original and stunning results. On the other hand, you may live in a modern building but like traditional interiors, in which case the addition of traditional moldings, reclaimed floorboards, or a cornice or frieze will automatically transport a room into a different period. Your choice of sofa, pictures, and other details, such as lamp shades and curtains, will further enhance the style of the whole interior.

The living room is an area where it is best to avoid too many sharp edges and hard lines. Soft curves and rounded objects allow you to relax more easily and feel comfortable. The idea of softness can be extended into the area of lighting. Low-level lighting through the use of lamps, as opposed to overhead lighting, is one way of creating a warm and gentle atmosphere. A circuit arrangement that allows you to switch on all the lamps together in combination with a dimmer switch is an invaluable means of creating the desired mood. If there is a fireplace, make the best of it by using it as the central feature of the room, rather than the television.

I find it helpful to seek inspiration from nature. I based the design of my living room on the colors of a honeysuckle plant. I painted the walls in a warm, golden yellow that positively glowed in the evening light. I painted the wooden floor in a green that matched the green of the leaves and stems, and added accents and details, such as rugs, cushions, and candles, in the beautiful magenta and deep pinks found in the petals. I am constantly looking for delicious and unusual color combinations, and if you let nature be your guide you cannot really go wrong. Do, however, notice the proportions in which the colors appear in relation to each other and look at the whole rather than zooming in on a detail. Colors look very different when they are all over your walls.

There are a wealth of color possibilities to consider when designing a living room, which needs to create a mood that is supportive of both rest and the pursuit of leisure activities. Consider which objects, styles, cultures, or landscapes you are drawn to. For some, it may be the neutral hues and textures of untreated wood or stone, which create an uncluttered, almost Zen-like sense of calm and peace. Others may seek to withdraw into tranquil and spacious sea blues and greens, warmed up with gold or shades of coral. For still others, the living room may be a place that is more dramatic and theatrical: an area where sensual textiles and a sense of luxury and pampering pervades. In this case, rich, jewel-colored walls, windows hung with sumptuous velvet drapes, thick-pile rugs, and exotic, embroidered cushions can all help to transport the mind to far-off places.

The choice of colors employed depends entirely on the atmosphere that you personally wish to create. However, it is also worth keeping in mind that most living areas are shared by all members of the family, so a neutral background color may be the easiest way of pleasing everybody.

Try to limit your palette to no more than two main colors, as well as a balancing or contrasting tone. A mixture of colors and styles can create a chaotic and incongruous effect, because the colors battle for attention, which is not conducive to relaxation. Variety of color is best introduced here in the form of paintings, sofa covers, curtains, cushions, plants, and ornaments.

Colors to avoid in a living room are flat grays or blacks, violent shades of violet or purple, and acidic yellows and greens. White can look wonderful, but it is best to choose a slightly off-white tone to keep the effect from becoming too cold and isolating.

Natural matte finishes are good for large surfaces because they reflect light and color more softly than even slightly shiny walls, and the result is a warm and restful effect. As with the dining area, you may need to forgo this pleasure in areas that receive more wear and tear, but the ceiling, at least, can be matte.

THE BATHROOM

This is often the room that is given the least attention in terms of design and size, and yet a beautiful bathroom can add so much quality to our daily life. In earlier times, bathing was very much a social occasion, and considerable time was spent on the processes of cleansing, relaxing, invigorating, and pampering the body. Spas are the last remnants of this approach and are still seen as the ultimate luxury. With a little imagination, however, we can create a bathing haven within our own home.

On the most basic level, a bathroom serves the essential function of hygiene. This is where we wash ourselves. Unlike many of the other rooms in a house, it is the room in which we are generally alone. It is also the room that sees us naked and, in some ways, slightly vulnerable.

The main element featuring in a bathroom is water. We are made up of 80 percent water, so we have a natural affinity with this element. Symbolically, water represents life, and in religions all around the world water is seen as having a purifying power not only on our bodies but also on our souls. Many important ceremonies take place by or in water, such as the rite of baptism, so in a symbolic sense, at least, the bathroom is an extremely important room. The time we spend in it can be turned into quality time through simple and inexpensive ideas.

Far left: Warm, sunlit oranges give an impression of cozy intimacy.
Left: Cool blues and greens create an atmosphere of austere simplicity.

Wicker screens and imitation animal skins
suggest safari trips and heat waves.

This bathroom is perfectly suited to its urban setting, with steps and surfaces that reflect in miniature the view from the window.

Lighting is of great importance in the bathroom. Light bulbs that tend toward the yellow or pink end of the spectrum can help transform any bathroom into a supportive and healing environment, a place in which to feel comfortable with our body. Bright or harsh lights that tend toward the blue tones are unflattering and ruthless on the skin, an effect not appreciated in a room that generally contains mirrors. A semitransparent blind or light muslin curtain to diffuse the daylight is ideal for creating soft light, while candles can be used in the evening to create a lovely warm effect.

Have a range of delicious-smelling essential oils or soaps to choose from: They transform an ordinary bath into a spa experience, regenerating the mind, body, and spirit in their own individual ways. Different aromatic oils can also be used specifically to create a certain mood or to help when you are suffering from common ailments. Ylang-ylang oil, for example, evokes a rich, sensual atmosphere, while lavender oil creates a soothing, healing ambience. Plants, such as ferns, can increase the natural feel of the room, while the inclusion of objects like stones, shells, and driftwood collected on vacation also

encourages relaxation and leads the mind away from daily routines.

Sea motifs are always popular with children. Apart from using the bathroom to display found treasures, the color scheme can also pick up the theme of the ocean. Turquoise can be an excellent color to use in a bathroom, giving it a pure, clean, light atmosphere. Combined with white fixtures, it can look minty and fresh, especially when it tends toward the green tones. This is also a great choice of color if you are a sports enthusiast and use the bathroom to shower, since it has a cooling and relaxing effect on the body.

To create a sumptuous atmosphere in which to nourish the senses and pamper the body, choose the richer Mediterranean blues, such as cobalt or aquamarine. In cooler climates, however, all blue shades may be too cold in winter, so warmer colors can be added via the curtains, tiles, towels, and accessories. Soft mauve or violet tones have a gentle warmth and coordinate well with cream units or accessories. Alternatively, warm peach tones help to create an attractive space in which to remove your clothes, giving the skin a healthy glow. Pink, peach, and rose tones also help to relax the muscles and create a sense of safety and nurturing.

Many people are now choosing to have the bathroom incorporated into the main bedroom, possibly separated by a partition or screen. In this case, the colors and style of the bedroom will largely dictate those of the bathroom.

Casein paint is not an option in a steamy bathroom, but a lime paint will self-regulate its moisture content—darkening in color as it absorbs steam and becoming paler again as it dries—so it could be used, but not in those areas that are in direct contact with water. Ecopaints, especially those with a satin finish, are highly suitable for the bathroom.

THE BEDROOM

The bedroom is a place in which it is essential to feel safe and at peace. When a person is asleep, it is easy to think how innocent and defenseless they look. While we sleep, our bodies are performing important functions to prepare us for the activities of the following day. On a psychological level, it is the place where we process the events and feelings of the previous day and receive inspiration and ideas for the next day. Apart from providing a restful and safe environment in which to sleep, the bedroom is also a place for making love. What makes a room conducive to relaxation, safety, and intimacy?

Ideally, the bedroom should be located in a place away from a road or other noise, and should face east or southeast to receive the morning sun. For those who have problems waking up in the mornings, it is best to have thin curtains that allow the natural dawn light to filter through. For those with sleeping difficulties, or if help is needed to deaden noise levels, heavier curtains that block out the light are more appropriate. Lighting in the bedroom does not need to be very bright. A pair of good bedside reading lamps are probably the only bright lights you will need. Lights tending more toward the blue end of the spectrum will have a calming effect on the mind and body.

Men and women tend to differ enormously in their taste of bedroom design, but a few general guidelines can help to avoid using colors that are likely to have an adverse effect on sleep. Reds and oranges are best used in places where their stimulating effect can be transformed into activity. Blue can encourage relaxation but also detachment through its cooling effect. Bright yellows are cheerful but also promote intellectual activity and are therefore to be avoided in the bedroom, especially if you suffer from insomnia. Cream, soft green, peach, rose, salmon, and plum are all tones of color that offer support, tranquility, and emotional nurturing through the night. If your bedroom is also somewhere you like to meditate, any shade of lilac or lavender can help to evoke a sense of calm, and encourage contact with the spiritual side of life. Crimsons and magentas, on the other hand, like reds and orange, will encourage and stimulate sexual activity.

Paint for bathroom surfaces must be chosen carefully, whatever style of bathroom you choose.

Above and below: A restful atmosphere can be achieved in a bedroom by sticking to one color throughout.

Do not mix too many paint colors together in the bedroom; the effect will not be restful. Interest and variety may be introduced in the colors of the sheets, bedcovers, curtains, lamp shades, or paintings.

It is possible to encourage the flow of energy around a house or apartment through the careful use of color. In order to prevent each room from being completely isolated from the others, it is a good idea to take some of the colors or elements of one room into the next. This idea does not have to be restricted to just paint, however. You can use any objects to create such color or style links.

Just imagine a smooth transition from one room to another, and discover your own way of getting the energy flowing around your home.

An adult bedroom is probably the perfect low-wearing situation in which to experience the beauty of casein paint or size-base paint.

My bedroom color scheme (see right) was based on the old-looking pinks I saw first in the hollyhocks outside my front door, and subsequently in the interiors of an old Spanish villa pictured in an interior design magazine. To keep the pink from becoming too sickly, I brought in deep burgundy colors in the cushions, candles, and paintings, and fresh green plants. The doors are old paneled ones with small grooves around the panels. Using a small brush, I

Left: An embroidered throw adds a touch of luxury to a bedroom.

Above and left: Flowers, especially scented varieties, can introduce sensuality into a bedroom.

painted just these grooves and those on the door frames with a burgundy color, thereby allowing the energy from the bedroom to flow out into the hallway. This continued into the study, complementing the turquoise color of the walls in a subtle way.

Angela Findlay
Color therapist

CHILDREN'S ROOMS

By its very nature, a child's room is going to change with time. A typical baby's room may contain a frieze of bunnies or bears, and a mobile above the crib. A few years later, the bears will be changed to spaceships or horses. As children start to customize their own space, posters of pop stars, dolphins, cars, and football players cover the walls. By the time they are 15, you might find that every surface in the room is covered with knick-knacks and bits of electronic hardware.

We need, therefore, to approach the design for a child's room knowing that change should be embraced. Young babies are not going to assess the style of their decor; all they really want is to feel safe and secure. If we imagine where they have been, inside the womb, experiencing the rhythmical sounds of the mother's heartbeat and surrounded by warmth, softness, and darkness, we can also imagine the incredible contrast with the outside world, with its hardness, coldness, and bright lights. So the bedroom where a baby spends its first months needs to simulate the womb. Soft drapes over the window will create a gentle light, and walls painted in layers of a pale but warm pink or peach blossom will create warm surroundings. It is best to keep the decor simple at this stage, with less-defined motifs for the baby to assimilate.

Casein paint is good for a baby's room—completely safe, natural, and odor-free. You could protect the diaper-changing area with a glaze. Once the child is mobile, durability needs to come into the equation, but it would be fine to paint over the casein with a satin ecopaint.

As they grow up, children need two types of space: somewhere small, intimate, secret, and cozy— a place of calm, a sanctuary—and somewhere to run, shout, build, and develop. To quote Christopher Alexander in *The Pattern Language*, "If children do not have space to release tremendous amounts of energy when they need to, they will drive themselves and everybody else in the family up the wall."

How can we combine these two demands in a room for a growing child? The ideal would be a small room opening onto a larger space; nearly as good would be as large a room as possible, where divisions could be made between different areas. One ingenious and appealing idea is to place the bed on a platform raised off the ground. The space underneath can then be used as part toy storage and part secret cave or den. It may be enclosed with curtains to add a further element of mystery. Later, as the child grows, the space under the bed can become a versatile storage area with the addition of a hanging rail.

I had the idea to raise my bed above floor level because my room is in the attic and there was a lot of wasted space in the roof. I like the idea of having my bed off the ground because it is fun...it is like having a little den up there. As it is quite a small room, it also means that I have more space underneath the bed where I can keep my clothes. I wanted colorwashed walls because I like the effect and I chose warm saffron/terra-cotta colors to make it feel cozy. I love India, so many of the things in my room have an Eastern theme (see picture bottom right).
Natasha Lawless, age 13

The larger space needs open shelving and work surfaces for homework and projects. As the child grows, the surface height can be raised. There could also be flexible lighting, varying from bright to subdued.

What kinds of decoration and color schemes are supportive of such a range of activities and requirements? The effect we should try to create is one of no boundaries in order to stimulate a child's individuality. Leonardo da Vinci spoke of the suggestive power of unmotivated random marks on walls to stimulate the creative imagination. Children spend many hours dreaming in their rooms, so why not give them surfaces to drift into?

Colorwashed walls, which have depth and a sense of spaciousness, encourage

creativity. Subtly textured effects with paint and color, such as sponged or rag-rolled walls, are also suitable for children's rooms. Above all, the effect needs to be gentle, transparent, and soft. As time goes by, other layers can be added to the walls to strengthen the effect and to cover the inevitable wear and tear of a hard-working room.

Younger children need a space that supports innovative and imaginative activity within a warm and reassuringly secure, dreamy environment. The colors that encourage these feelings are the soft, washed-out terra-cottas to warm pinks. Early teens, on the other hand, need environments that support the internalization of outer activity and the development of the intellect—the color range for this would be cool blue or yellows. Natural light and the colors of adjoining rooms should temper the strength and depth of the colors.

Many teenagers want to paint their rooms in strong primary colors, or sometimes black. Black serves as a cloak behind which the new identity of the young adult can begin to form, and creates a boundary between the child and the outside world. As a teenager, when new emotions are being discovered, sometimes with great discomfort, this protection can be an aid. Primary colors, on the other hand, stimulate emotional responses and clearly express something about who we are.

Whatever the case, parents can support their children through these formative years by encouraging them to express themselves through color, and by respecting their need to explore different avenues of their being.

Children's bedrooms are multipurpose. Each of the bedrooms pictured here combines an open area for play with an enclosed space for sleep or rest.

Appendix

COMMERCIAL PRODUCTS

Store-bought natural paints are sometimes very similar to the simple recipes in chapter 3. Others are more sophisticated combinations of ingredients, often based on traditional recipes but carefully formulated for reliable top-quality performance. Some of the ingredients contained in ready-made natural paints should be familiar to you, along with the role that they play in the recipe. Here we take a closer look at the labels to see how basic paint recipes have been adapted with a variety of ingredients in order to improve some of their desirable qualities.

In the following pages you will find some descriptions of the raw materials that you might find listed on the labels of commercial natural paints and finishes so that, should you prefer not to mix all of your own products, you will still know more about what has gone into the recipe.

POSSIBLE INGREDIENTS IN CASEIN PAINT

Binders

CASEIN
Dried milk curd/protein. Has strong adhesive qualities, especially when mixed with an alkali such as lime.

LIME
Produced from calcium carbonate.

CELLULOSE
The principal structural molecular component of plant cell walls, and the most abundant organic compound on Earth. Cellulose is composed of very long chains of glucose molecules, which are insoluble in water and are intertwined and super-coiled. Produced industrially from wood pulp, cellulose is used as a binder in its own right, but also swells into a jelly when mixed with

water, so it acts as a thickening agent to help keep all the other ingredients dispersed in the mix. Methyl cellulose is chemically decomposed wood cellulose.

Fillers

CALCIUM CARBONATE
Very common mineral, which is the major constituent of many of the Earth's rocks, and occurs in various forms such as calcite, chalk, and limestone. Calcium carbonate is composed of the fossilized skeletal remains of minute marine animals. Also used to produce lime.

CHALK
Fine-grained white rock consisting largely of calcium carbonate, similar to limestone but softer. Chalk is finely ground to be used as a filler and also as a white pigment.

CHINA CLAY/KAOLIN
One of the purest, whitest, and most plastic clays. Also used to make porcelain.

CLAYS
Silicate clays are natural minerals that have a capacity for expansion. They are therefore used as thixotropic agents in hydrous and resin oil products.

POWDERED MARBLE
Marble rises as a result of the action of heat and pressure on limestone. It has a hard, crystalline texture.

TALCUM (MAGNESIUM SULFATE)
Used as another thixotropic filler, i.e., it is used to hold other ingredients in suspension, and improves adhesion and coverage.

Pigment

EARTH PIGMENTS
Probably white, to improve the level of opacity in the basic mix.

POSSIBLE INGREDIENTS IN ECOPAINT

Binders

CELLULOSE/METHYL CELLULOSE
(See ingredients in casein paint.)

COLOPHONY GLYCEROL ESTER
A hard, brittle, translucent material obtained by steam distillation from crude turpentine resin, which is exuded from coniferous trees. The trees are milked similar to the way rubber trees are milked for latex. The liquid part of the crude resin is used as oil of turpentine, or turps. The resin is then boiled down with glycerol to make a more elastic material.

DAMMAR
Very light and non-yellowing transparent tree resin. Sap is harvested in a sustainable fashion from the meranti tree (*Agathis/Shorea*) and used as a highly elastic binder. It is soluble in alcohol and turpentine.

LINSEED STAND OIL
A thick oil made by heating linseed (from crushed flaxseed, *Linum usitatissimum*) oil to temperatures of 600°F (315°C) and higher. Linseed stand oil dries more quickly than raw linseed oil and is used both as an elastic binder and as a drier.

REZINE STAND OIL
Dehydrated castor oil, made from the seeds of the Christ palm tree (*Ricinus communis*). Used as a highly viscous binder and drier. Castor oil softens, prevents yellowing, and improves adhesion of paint.

Solvents and emulsifiers

LECITHIN
Commercially made from soybeans, peanuts, and corn. A gel-like product, used as an emulsifier and stabilizer in paints and also in foods.

ORANGE OIL
Essential oil used as a thinner.
(See D-limonene under
ingredients in eggshell and gloss
paints.)

PLANT ALCOHOL
Ethanol. Produced by the
fermentation of starchy plants.
Used as a thinner.

VINEGAR ESTER
Solvent made from the distillation
of vinegar.

Fillers

ALUMINUM SILICATE
White mineral. Clay consists
essentially of hydrous aluminum
silicates mixed with other
substances.

CHALK
(See ingredients in casein paint.)

KALKSPAR
Calc spar, or calcite. (See calcium
carbonate, under ingredients in
casein paint.)

KAOLIN
(See ingredients in casein paint.)

POWDERED MARBLE
(See ingredients in casein paint.)

SILICATE CLAY
(See ingredients in casein paint.)

TALCUM
(See ingredients in casein paint.)

Other ingredients

BORATES
Naturally occurring alkaline
minerals.

EUCALYPTUS OIL
Scented essential oil with
antibacterial properties.

ROSEMARY OIL (*Rosmarinus
officinalis*)
Scented essential oil with mild
fungicidal and preservative
properties.

SODIUM HYDROXIDE
An alkaline water-softening salt,
industrially produced by the
electrolysis of brine.

TITANIUM DIOXIDE
An expensive bright white
pigment. Used widely and valued
for its high opacity.

POSSIBLE INGREDIENTS IN A GLAZE OR COLORWASH MEDIUM

Binders

CARNAUBA WAX
Yellowish wax extracted from the
leaves of the fan palm (*Copernicia
cerifera*). The tree secretes the
wax to prevent excess
evaporation from its leaves, as a
defense against the hot winds
and droughts of its native habitat
in Brazil. This coating is removed
by drying and flailing. Carnauba is
the hardest natural wax with the
highest melting point known. Its
particular hardness is sometimes
used to increase the stability of
softer waxes.

CELLULOSE/METHYL
CELLULOSE
(See ingredients in casein paint.)

Solvents and emulsifiers

VINEGAR ESTER
(See ingredients in ecopaint.)

Fillers

CLAYS
(See ingredients in casein paint.)

KIESELGUHR
Form of silica composed of the
siliceous shells of unicellular
aquatic plants of microscopic size
(algae). It is used as a diffusion-
enhancing, matting filler and
suspension agent.

SILICIC ACID
Silicon dioxide extracted from
sand or quartz, used as a
hardener and gloss flattener or
matting agent. A reinforcing filler,
it imparts burnish resistance and
sheen uniformity.

POSSIBLE INGREDIENTS IN EGGSHELL OR GLOSSY PAINT

Binders

COLOPHONY
(See ingredients in ecopaint.)

LINSEED OIL
Drying oil (an oil that, in the
presence of air, dries to form a
dry, tough, durable, elastic skin)
extracted from linseed or flax.
(See ingredients in ecopaint.)

METHYL CELLULOSE
(See ingredients in casein paint.)

RICINUS OIL
Castor oil (see ingredients in
ecopaint).

SOY-BASED ALKYD
Synthetic resin derived from the
renewable resource of soybeans.
An alkyd resin is made by
reacting a drying oil (an oil that, in
the presence of air, dries to form
a dry, tough, durable, elastic skin)
with a hard, synthetic material.

SUNFLOWER OIL
Extracted from the seeds of the
sunflower (*Helianthus annuus*).
Used as a quality, non-yellowing
oil in paints.

Solvents and emulsifiers

D-LIMONENE
A citrus terpene, the principal
constituent of orange essential
oil, which is extracted from
orange peel by cold-pressing and
steam distillation. It is used as a
solvent in paints and cleaning
products.

ISOALIPHATE
Isomeric aliphatic hydrocarbon
derivative of natural gas. Solvent
of low odor and toxicity.

SOY LECITHIN
(See ingredients in ecopaint.)

Fillers

CHALK
(See ingredients in casein paint.)

Appendix

CLAYS
(See ingredients in casein paint.)

DOLOMITE
A light mineral, calcium magnesium carbonate.

POWDERED MARBLE
(See ingredients in casein paint.)

SILICIC ACID
(See ingredients in a glaze and colorwash medium.)

Driers

COBALT
Metallic element, used in small amounts as a powerful "active" drier. Acts primarily as an oxidation catalyst and encourages the hardening of the surface of the paint film. Generally used in combination with "secondary driers," such as zirconium, which encourage polymerization of the binder. Thus there is a combination of a hard-wearing surface with a more flexible body of paint underneath, which will move with the wood.

ZINC AND ZIRCONIUM SALTS
Secondary driers, or desiccants.

Other ingredients

BORATES
(See ingredients in ecopaint.)

GLYCERINE ESTER
By-product of the splitting of oils to produce solid stearic acids. These oils could be of animal (tallow) or plant (palm oil) origin.

TITANIUM DIOXIDE
(See ingredients in ecopaint.)

XANTHAN
Gum produced by the micro-organism *Xanthamonas campestris*. Used as a thickener and stabilizer in paints and foods.

OTHER POSSIBLE INGREDIENTS IN STORE-BOUGHT NATURAL PAINTS AND FINISHES

BALSAMIC TURPENTINE
Distilled from pine oleoresin, which is "milked" from living trees. A volatile oil, used as a solvent. (See Colophony, under ingredients in ecopaint.)

BEESWAX
Easily obtainable, supple wax with a long tradition of use in many parts of the world. Female worker honeybees secrete a clear liquid from glands on the underside of their abdomens. This liquid hardens upon contact with the air to form a white wax— the yellow color comes from its pollen content—and they use this to build their honeycombs.

COPAL RESIN
Hard tropical tree resin related to amber. Dissolved in alcohol to make varnishes. Also used as incense and meditation aid.

NATURAL LATEX
Not to be confused with synthetic, petrochemical-derived, "latex" paints. Natural latex is made from a milky substance that drips from the rubber tree (*Hevea brasiliensis*) when the bark is slashed. A natural rubber, used as a permanently elastic binder.

SHELLAC
Resin-like secretion of a tiny parasitic scale insect (*Laccifer lacca*); the secretion is used to protect its young. Harvested by scraping the crust of resin off the twigs or by cutting off the twigs (stick lac). This is ground, washed, and dried, and then dissolved in alcohol to make a varnish.

TUNG OIL
Obtained from the seeds of the poisonous fruits of the tung tree, which grows in China and Japan. Tung oil is used as a quick-drying binder in paints and varnishes.

Recommended Reading

Baker, Paula,
Erica Elliott, and John Banta
**Prescriptions for a
Healthy House**
New Society, 2002

Carson, Rachel
Silent Spring
Penguin Books,
2000 (New Edition)

Chiras, Daniel
The Natural House
Chelsea Green, 2000

Chiazzira, Suzy
Healing Home
Ebury Press, 2000

Lao Tzu, Stephen Mitchell
(Translator)
Tao-te Ching
Kyle Cathie, 2000 (New Edition)

Lovelock, James
**GAIA: New Look at Life on
Earth**
Oxford Paperbacks,
1992 (New Edition)

McCloud, Kevin
**Kevin McCloud's
Decorating Book**
Ebury Press, 1999

Pearson, David
The Natural House Book
Gaia Books, 2000

Rousseau, David
**Your Home, Your Health,
and Well Being**
Ten Speed Press, 1988

Schumacher, E. F.
Small is Beautiful
Vintage, 1993 (Reissue)

Resources

Antique Drapery Rod Co. Inc.
140 Glass Street
Dallas, TX 75207
Tel: (214) 653 1733
Website:
www.antiquedraperyrod.com

Online retailer of milk paints and natural wax sealers, as well as reproduction accessories for the home.

Aqua Oleum
Lower Wharf
Wallbridge
Stroud
Gloucestershire GL5 3JA
UK
Tel: 01453 753 555
Website: www.aqua-oleum.co.uk

Mail order suppliers of high quality essential oils and vegetable oils.

Auro Natural Paints and Finishes
1340-G Industrial Avenue
Petaluma, CA 94952
Tel: (707) 763 0662
Toll Free: (888) 302 9352
Fax: (707) 769 7342
Email: info@aurousa.com
Website: www.aurousa.com

Mailorder supplier of the full range of Auro products.

Building for Health – Materials Centre
PO Box 113
Carbondale, CO 81623
Tel: (970) 963 0437
Fax: (970) 963 3318
Email:
contactus@buildingsforhealth.com
Website:
www.buildingforhealth.com
Toll Free: (800) 292 4838

Supplier of ecofriendly building materials, appliances and home comforts.

Eco Design Company
1330 Rufina Circle
Santa Fe, NM 87507
Tel: (505) 438 3448
Toll Free: (800) 621 2591
Fax: (505) 438 0199
Email: edesignco@aol.com
Website: www.bioshieldpaint.com

Supplier of natural paints, stains, finishes, and cleaners.

Eco-House Inc.
PO Box 220
STN A
Fredericton NB E3B 4YN
Canada
Tel: 506 366 3529
Fax: 506 366 3577
Email: henry@eco-house.com
Website:www.eco-house.com

Canadian retailer of artists mediums, solvents, thinners, and woodfinishes made from natural and nontoxic ingredients. Also, see website for extensive directory of Canadian, US and New Zealand retailers.

Ecovillage Network of Canada Reseau d'Ecovillage du Canada
6080 Lake Ridge Rd.
Uxbridge Ont. L9P 1R4
Canada
Email: tycoed@attcanada.ca

Forum for exchange of ideas and information on healthy, sustainable living in our homes and daily lives, and for promotion of ecovillage concepts and practices.

Fine Paints of Europe
PO Box 419
Route 4 West
Woodstock, VT 05091-0419
Tel: (802) 457-2468
Toll Free: (800) 332 1556
Fax: (802) 457-3984
Website: www.finepaints.com

Retailer of natural paints and equipment for decorative paint effects.

The Gilders Warehouse Ltd
5 & 4D Woodside Commercial
Estate
Thornwood
Epping
Essex CM16 6LJ
UK
Tel: 01992 570 453
Email:
alias@gilders-warehouse.co.uk
Website:
www.gilders-warehouse.co.uk

Mail order suppliers of raw materials for paint making including casein, whiting, oils, waxes, gums and glues.

Heaton Cooper Studio
Grasmere
Cumbria LA22 9SX
UK
Tel: 01539 435 280
Email: sales@heatoncooper.co.uk
Website:
www.heatoncooper.co.uk

Mail order suppliers of raw materials including oils, glues and natural solvents. Also color wheels.

Old Fashioned Milk Paint Company
436 Main Street
PO Box 222
Groton, MA 01450
Tel: (978) 448 6336
Fax: (978) 448 2754
Email: Anne@milkpaint.com
Website: www.milkpaint.com

Suppliers of traditional paint made from milk protein, quicklime, and earth pigments.

Sawyer Finn Natural Paint Company
1600 Genessee Street
Suite 555
Kansas City, MO 64102
Tel/Fax: (816) 421 4717
Website: www.sawyerfinn.com

Online supplier of milk paint.

Sepp Leaf Products, Inc.
381 Park Avenue South
New York, NY 10016
Tel: (212) 683-2840
Fax: (212) 725-0308
Website: www.seppleaf.com

Retailer of gold and silver leaf.

Sinan Company
PO Box 857
Davis, CA 95617-0857
Tel: (530) 753-3104
Email: sinan@dcn.davis.ca.us

Retailer of natural paints and
pigments.

Tried & True Wood Finishes
14 Prospect Street
Trumansburg, NY 14886
Tel: (607) 387 9280
Website:
www.triedandtruewoodfinish.com

Traditional producers and retailers
of linseed-oil finishes.

Index

Index

Acknowledgments

Authors' Acknowledgments

Thanks go to Roger Budgeon for the provision of time, space, and facilities to write—also to Bruce Walker. The expertise of Angela Findlay, Alan Beaven, and Steve Niner is appreciated.

John and Marianne Downs, and Tara, for their generous natures and for the use of their home during the practical photography shoots. Thanks also to Sheila York and Heather Brown for her inspirational photography.

Special appreciation to Martyn Mason for his input in so many aspects of this book, from his broad-ranging historical and practical knowledge about the subject, to the hard physical work involved in the photo shoots. Also for personal encouragement and support throughout.

Thanks are also due to Judy Allan, Natasha Lawless, Anne Marie Robinson, Maciek Sikora, Dorothee von Grieff, and all at Kyle Cathie Ltd.

Color consultant and therapist:
Angela Findlay
angelafindlay@insidecolours.freese
rve.co.uk
44-7881-526 925

Feng Shui consultant:
Maciek Sikora
contact.magic@virgin.net
44-7773-393 009

Natural Interiors consultant:
Martyn Mason
48 Horns Road
Stroud
Gloucestershire
GL5 1ED
England
44-1453-758 625

Photographer:
Heather Brown
117 Belgrave Road
Darwen
Lancashire
BB3 2SF
England
44-1254-761 381

Publisher's Acknowledgments

Thanks to the following for their kind permission to reproduce images:

5 Ray Main/Mainstream; 6 *top* Andrew Wood/The Interior Archive; 7 *left* Ray Main/Mainstream; 8 Caves of Lascaux, Dordogne, France/Bridgeman Art Library; 9 ANT/NHPA; 10 Caves of Lascaux, Dordogne, France/Bridgeman Art Library; 11 *left to right* B. Norman/Ancient Art and Architecture and Georgia Glynn-Smith/Garden Picture Library; 12 (Copyright The British Museum); 13 Mary Jelliffe/Ancient Art and Architecture; 14 Ray Main/Mainstream/Designer Drew Plunkett; 16–17 Museo e Gallerie Nazionali di Capodimonte/Bridgeman Art Library; 18 Herbert Ypma/The Interior Archive; 19 *left to right* By permission of The British Library (ROY.6.E. folio 329 min.) and Lawrence Engelsberg/Swift Imagery; 20 Malachite (The Natural History Museum); 21 Michael Leach/NHPA; 22 James Carmichael Junior/NHPA; 23 Lead ore (The Natural History Museum); 24 *top to bottom* BBC Natural History Unit, Lapis lazuli (The Natural History Museum and Howard Rice/Garden Picture Library); 25 *left to right* Lead (The Natural History Museum and Dorothy Burrows/Swift Imagery); 26 Jany Sauvanet/NHPA; 29 *sunflower* Densey Clyne/Garden Picture Library; *linseed* Guy Edwardes/NHPA; *poppies* BBC Natural History Unit, Lead (The Natural History Museum); *reseda* Ros Wickham/Garden Picture Library; 32 Ray Main/Mainstream; 39 Elizabeth Whiting and Associates; 47 Ray Main/Mainstream; 92 *top to bottom* Elizabeth Whiting and Associates; Nick Todd/Elizabeth Whiting and Associates; Gill Wyatt-Smith/Elizabeth Whiting and Associates; Earl/Elizabeth Whiting and Associates; 93 Ray Main/Mainstream/Architect Charles Rutherford; 140–141 Simon McBride/The Interior Archive; 142 Andrew Dee/Abode; 144 Ray Main/Mainstream/Architect Charles Rutherford; 145 Simon McBride/The Interior Archive; 146 Painter: Fleur Kelly (44-1373-814651/ www.fleurkelly.com/ info@fleurkelly.com). Site: Health Center, Voyager of the Seas, Royal Caribbean International. Photographer: Fotek.; 147 Simon McBride/The Interior Archive; 148 Ray Main/Mainstream; 149 Ray Main/Mainstream; 150 Ray Main/Mainstream; 151 Ray Main/Mainstream; 153 Ray Main/Mainstream; 156 *left* Ray Main/Mainstream; 157 *middle and bottom* Ray Main/Mainstream/Architects McDowel & Benedetti; Ray Main/Mainstream; 158 Ray Main/Mainstream; 161 Ray Main/Mainstream; 162 Ray Main/Mainstream/ Designer Oriana Fielding Banks; 163 *left and right* Ray Main/Mainstream; 165 Ray Main/Mainstream; 166 Ray Main/Mainstream; 168 *left and right* Ray Main/Mainstream; 169 Ray Main/Mainstream/Designer Gianni Cinnali; 170 Ray Main/Mainstream; 172 Ray Main/Mainstream/Architect Spencer Fung; 173 *left to right* Ray Main/Mainstream and Andrew Wood/The Interior Archive; 174 Andrew Wood/The Interior *bottom* Ray Main/Mainstream/LTS Architects, Ray Main/Mainstream/Mulberry and Ray Main/Mainstream; 179 *right* Ray Main/Mainstream; 180–181 *young girl* Edina van der Wyck/The Interior Archive; *yellow bedroom* Tony Hall/Abode; *flowers* Francesca Yorke